rororo sprachen
Herausgegeben von Ludwig Moos

Das Telefon läutet – irgendein Engländer, Amerikaner, Kanadier oder Japaner überfällt Sie mit einem englischen Wortschwall. Oder Ihr Chef läßt Sie in einer heiklen Sache bei einem ausländischen Partner anrufen. Keine Panik! *How to Phone Effectively* vermittelt Ihnen mit Pfiff, Witz und Ironie das notwendige Telefonenglisch für alle typischen Situationen, von A wie Absagen bis Z wie Zimmerbuchung. Spielerisch lernen Sie Teletactics: Wie beginnt man ein Gespräch, wie bricht man es ab, wie dringt man zu den wichtigen Leuten durch, wie bremst man einen Schnellredner, wie verschafft man sich Gewißheit? So gewinnen Sie die Phone Power, mit der Sie sich und Ihre Produkte am Telefon verkaufen können. Die Toncassette zum Buch (60146) oder die Audio-CD im Buch (60147) verrät, wie sich das alles anhört, und schult im Sprechen.

Dr. René Bosewitz ist Native Speaker und unterrichtet an der Berufsakademie Mannheim. In einer deutschen Zweigstelle der London Chamber of Commerce bereitet er Firmenangehörige auf einschlägige sprachliche Prüfungen vor. Er trainiert zudem seit vielen Jahren Topmanager aus Banken und Industrie in Business English. Mit Robert Kleinschroth hat er bei rororo sprachen *Joke Your Way through English Grammar* (8527) und *Joke by Joke to Conversation* (8795) veröffentlicht.

Robert Kleinschroth unterrichtet Englisch am Gymnasium und an der Universität Heidelberg. Er hat zwanzig Jahre Praxis in der Erwachsenenbildung und leitete fünfzehn Jahre lang die Sprachabteilung eines Großunternehmens. Robert Kleinschroth hat zusammen mit Dieter Maupai *La Grammaire en s'amusant* (8714) verfaßt und außerdem *La Conversation en s'amusant* (8873) sowie *Sprachen lernen* (9140), *Sprachen lernen mit dem Computer* (9520) und *Neues Lernen mit dem Computer* (9841) geschrieben.

In der Reihe *Business English* sind von beiden Autoren außerdem erschienen: *Manage in English* (60137), *Better than the Boss* (60138), *Test Your Management Skills* (60260), *Get Through at Meetings* (60262), *Let's Go International* (60267) und *Check Your Language Level* (60268).

RENÉ BOSEWITZ / ROBERT KLEINSCHROTH

HOW TO PHONE EFFECTIVELY

BUSINESS ENGLISH
AM TELEFON

Rowohlt

rororo

Wir danken Frau Ortrud Grimm vielmals für ihre Hilfe
bei der Erstellung des Manuskripts.
Ohne sie hätten wir es wohl nicht geschafft.

16.–19. Tausend Januar 2000

Originalausgabe
Veröffentlicht im Rowohlt Taschenbuch Verlag GmbH,
Reinbek bei Hamburg, September 1996

Umschlaggestaltung Barbara Hanke
Illustration Cathrin Günther
Layout Anne Drude und Alexander Urban
Satz OCRA und Stone, QuarkXPress 3.31 (Dolev 800)
Druck und Bindung Clausen & Bosse, Leck
Printed in Germany
ISBN 3 499 60139 7

Inhalt

	Vorwort	6
	Gebrauchsanweisung	7
	Wegweiser	8
1	How it all began	11
2	Mr Brain places an advert	19
3	Defusing the angry customer	27
4	Suggestions and good advice	35
5	Screening off the boss	43
6	Getting around receptionists and secretaries	51
7	Through to the boss	59
8	A happy message	67
9	A job interview on the phone	73
10	Appointment with a potential customer	79
11	A ticket to Scotland	85
12	Can I take a message?	91
13	Shark is keen on Lizzy	97
14	Booking a room in Glasgow	103
15	Dinner for two	109
16	Andrew spreads his wings	115
17	Robot or Fussy – that is the question	121
18	Heading for the centre of the world	127
19	Straight into the lion's den	133
20	Robots to Germany	141
21	Robot runs riot	147
22	Epilogue: turning over a new page	155
	The complete thematic list of telefunctions	159
	Schlüssel zu den Übungen	183

Vorwort

Firmen investieren viel Geld in ihr Image. Doch den guten Eindruck, den ein Kunde hat, kann ungeschultes Telefonpersonal schnell zunichte machen. Ein unfreundlicher Ton, eine barsche Stimme, peinliche Mißverständnisse können negative Emotionen wecken. Sie schaden dem Firmenimage mehr als ein stilistisch schwacher Geschäftsbrief, der schnell vergessen ist. Die Telefonkultur Ihres Unternehmens ist ein wesentlicher Teil des Bildes, das Ihre Geschäftspartner von Ihnen gewinnen.

Was erwarten Sie von diesem Buch? Englisch für das Telefon, damit Sie nicht sprachlos sind, wenn ein japanischer Geschäftspartner am Apparat ist? Das dürfen Sie von uns erwarten, aber wir bieten noch mehr: Statt dürrer Dialoge ohne Zusammenhang finden Sie eine lockere Telefonstory um die Vermarktung von Heimrobotern. Dazu Übungen, die wir mit englischem Humor rund um das Telefon gewürzt haben. Darüber hinaus verhelfen drei weitere Bestandteile zur Telefonkompetenz.

Sprachkenntnisse (*Telefunctions* und *Speech functions*) sind beim Telefonieren unerläßlich, aber bei weitem nicht alles. Deshalb haben wir einen kleinen Knigge des Telefonierens (*Teletiquette*) eingestreut – auf Englisch, versteht sich, aber mit vielen Wortschatzhilfen. Unser psychologischer Ratgeber (*Your Teledoc*) klärt Sie über wichtige kommunikative Aspekte des Telefonierens auf. Wußten Sie zum Beispiel, wie man den Typ eines Menschen am Telefon erkennt und dessen Vertrauen gewinnt? Vielleicht noch wichtiger sind die Strategien und Taktiken des Telefonierens (*Teletactics*): Wie behandelt man verärgerte Kunden am Telefon? Wie schirmt man seinen Chef vor unerwünschten Vertretern ab? Wie dringt man trotz Sekretärin direkt zum Ohr des Chefs vor?

Natürlich schneiden wir auch das Thema Telefonmarketing an, schließlich wird heute so gut wie alles über das Telefon verkauft. Unsere Wegweiser zeigen Ihnen, wo Sie was finden.

Viel Spaß beim Telefonierenlernen.

Gebrauchsanweisung

1. Werfen Sie einen Blick auf einen der Telefondialoge. Kommt er Ihnen leicht verständlich vor? Wenn ja, dann sollten Sie vielleicht gleich Ihr Ohr schulen – falls Sie die Audio-CD oder Kassette erworben haben. Alle Texte auf dem Tonträger sind im Buch mit einem Telefonsymbol gekennzeichnet. Hören Sie sich die Dialoge kapitelweise an, und lesen Sie sie mit. Die Worthilfen am Rand ersparen Ihnen das Suchen in Wörterverzeichnissen. Hören Sie sich die Texte mehrmals an, bis Sie halblaut mitlesen oder nachsprechen können.
   Wenn Ihnen die Dialoge auf Anhieb nicht verständlich erscheinen, dann lesen Sie sie erst einmal und ziehen die Wortschatzangaben und die englisch-deutschen *Telefunctions* und *Speech functions* zu Rate.

2. Jedes Telefongespräch ist einem kleinen Bereich der Telefonsprache (*Telefunctions*) und anderer Redemittel des Geschäftslebens (*Speech functions*) gewidmet. Sie stehen unmittelbar nach dem Dialog und sind Lernstoff.

3. Anschließend machen Sie sich an die Übungen (*Your Teletrainer*). Im Anhang finden Sie die Lösungen.

4. Wenn Sie ein Kapitel durchgearbeitet haben, ist es Zeit, an die Aussprache- und Intonationsübungen auf der Audio-CD beziehungsweise auf der Kassette zu gehen. Arbeiten Sie mit der Pausentaste.

5. Im Anhang finden Sie ein nahezu komplettes Verzeichnis der Redewendungen in der Telefonsprache. Es ist sachlogisch und thematisch geordnet und soll Ihnen als Nachschlagewerk zur Vorbereitung auf Telefongespräche dienen.

1.	Anrufe entgegennehmen, sich melden	13, 159
2.	Anrufe machen: Sagen Sie, wer Sie sind	159
3.	Nennen Sie den Grund Ihres Anrufs	23, 60
4.	So identifizieren Sie den Anrufer	53, 132, 161
5.	Fragen Sie nach dem Grund des Anrufs	162
6.	Sagen Sie, wen Sie zu sprechen wünschen	61, 162
7.	Private Anrufe	39, 164
8.	So verbinden Sie Anrufer weiter	23, 24, 61, 164
9.	Anrufer auf Wartezeiten vorbereiten	23, 165
10.	Wie Sie Ungeduld und Verärgerung am Telefon äußern	28
11.	Wie Sie jemanden am Telefon unterbrechen	75, 167
12.	Entschuldigungen am Telefon	111, 167
13.	Ein Gespräch übergeben und übernehmen	167
14.	Was sagen Sie, wenn er/sie nicht erreichbar ist?	93, 168
15.	Nachrichten hinterlassen	69, 94, 169
16.	Nachrichten entgegennehmen	69, 70, 94, 169
17.	Nachrichten wiederholen und überprüfen	170
18.	Auf einem Telefontermin beharren	171
19.	So bitten Sie um einen Rückruf	171
20.	Sie rufen zurück. Was sagen Sie?	99, 172
21.	Sich für einen Rückruf bedanken	172
22.	Falsch verbunden	83, 173
23.	Der freundliche Gesprächsbeginn	99, 132, 172
24.	Was sagen Sie, wenn die Leitung schlecht ist?	83, 135
25.	Wie helfen Sie sich bei Verständigungs-schwierigkeiten?	105, 111, 136, 175
26.	Was sagen Sie, wenn Sie unter Zeitdruck stehen?	175
27.	So schirmen Sie Ihren Chef ab	46, 47, 61, 176
28.	So könnte Ihr Chef reagieren	177
29.	Ein Gespräch beenden	13, 53, 99, 112, 130, 176
30.	Anrufbeantworter und Ansagen	157, 178
31.	Bitten, ein privates Telefon benutzen zu dürfen	179
32.	Sie wollen ein öffentliches Telefon benutzen	179
33.	Hinweise in Telefonzellen	180
34.	Telefonieren im Postamt	180
35.	Anpiepsen und Faxen	181
36.	Wie buchstabiert man auf Englisch?	77, 182

Typische Situationen und ihre Redemittel

Chapter		
2	Trying to get information	23
3	The language of complaints	30, 149
4	Suggesting and advising	38, 117
7	Describing the way	63
8	Congratulating people	70
10	Making appointments	82
11	Booking things	88
14	Booking a room	105
15	Making excuses	111
17	Rearranging appointments	124
19	Praising employees	138
21	Making a complaint	30, 149

Teletactics: Strategien und Taktiken

1	"Hello" and "Goodbye" are not good enough	14
3	How to handle the angry customer	31, 153
5	Screening strategies	46, 47
6	Step by step to the Managing Director	53, 54
7	Avoiding rush hours and secretaries	65
7	Market studies on the phone	66
9	Spot the tactical mistake	77
12	Analysing the telephone conversation	77
13	Terminating calls effectively	112
14	Telephone marketing surpasses direct mail	105
15	How to avoid invitations	115
21	A dozen rules on how to handle complaints on the phone	150, 153

Teletiquette: Ein kleiner Knigge des Telefonierens

1	When not to use a company phone	14
2	How (not) to put someone through	23
2	Ten commandments for receptionists and secretaries	24
5	What to do if you can't put them through	50

8 One moment please, I'll get pencil and paper 70
9 Can you spell your name? 77
14 When not to call through a secretary 107
19 Telephone culture and time management 140
20 When portables don't come in handy 146
21 How to handle complaints on the phone 150

Your Teledoc: Verhaltenspsychologie im Telefongespräch

1 Don't panic when the phone rings 17
3 Create your image 34
4 Body language on the phone? 41
9 Why we interrupt 78
10 Getting to know the "visual" caller 84
11 Getting to know the "auditive" caller 90
12 Getting to know the "emotional" caller 108
16 Mirror the caller and win a friend 118
19 Don't interrupt – encourage 138
21 Don't sell them cars – sell them feelings 154
22 The first 20 seconds are the most important 156

HOW IT ALL BEGAN

CONTENTS

Our Telestory:	Mr Brain gets a phonecall from the boss
Telefunctions:	First and last words on the phone
Teletiquette:	When not to use the telephone
Your Teletrainer:	Practise your telefunctions
Teletactics:	"Hello" and "Goodbye" are not good enough
Your Teledoc:	Don't panic when the phone rings
Telejokes:	Humorous telephone dialogues

Let's start with a smile

I answer the phone "Dickerson here" because I am Dickerson and I am here. Now what the hell do you want, Martha?

Charles Basotti, Kings Don't Carry Money

How it all began

Once upon a time there was an engineer, Dr. Brian Brain, who had a very good job as a *research specialist* in the *Research and Development division* of a large and rather famous computer company, MBI. *Unfortunately* his work *bored* him, so *instead* of dealing with software and so on, he spent most of his time on his hobby, constructing a *sophisticated* robot. He made a large number of *inventions* and created a man-machine which was *capable* of doing a lot of things. Unfortunately the director of MBI *found out* about these extra activities. And he did not like it at all ...
(to be continued)

es war einmal
Forscher · Forschungsbereich
leider
langweilen · anstatt
hochentwickelt
Erfindungen
fähig
herausfinden
Fortsetzung folgt

A phone-call from the boss

Mrs Child, Department secretary (**S**), Mr Tickersun, the Boss (**T**), Dr. Brian Brain, an engineer (**B**).

S: Yes, R&D. Mrs Child speaking.
T: Tickersun here ...
S: Good morning, Mr Tickersun. Can I help you?
T: *You'd better*! That's what you're paid for. And stop *typing* when I'm speaking to you on the phone. Now where is Brain?
S: I'm afraid he isn't at his *desk*. He might be in the test *lab*. Shall I *page* him?
T: Do it, and quickly if you don't mind. *I've a plane to catch.*
(three minutes later)
B: Brain speaking. Can I be of help?

Sie täten gut daran
tippen
Schreibtisch
Labor · anpiepsen
ich muß ein Flugzeug erreichen

T: Be of help? Have you helped the company at all in the last six years? What exactly have you done? I mean what have you done for us? I'm not speaking about the computer work. *I'm referring* to your private work on *company time*: constructing robots.	*ich spreche von* *Arbeitszeit*
B: I'm sure I don't know what you mean. I always finish my work here before I do anything on my robot. *It's not my fault* if the work in the company doesn't *stretch* me enough.	*ich kann nichts dafür* *auslasten*
T: Oh, it doesn't stretch you, does it? And it doesn't stretch you to put your *salary* in your *pocket*, does it? Six years, is it? That's exactly how long you have been working here – *not including today* since you stopped working here five minutes ago. And *clear your desk by* Friday this week. Goodbye. *(to be continued)*	*Gehalt* *Tasche* *den heutigen Tag nicht mitgezählt* *räumen Sie Ihren Schreibtisch bis*

Telefunctions: First and last words on the phone

At the office: Hello ...

Robotalot. Good morning.	Firma Robotalot. Guten Morgen.
Who is (that) speaking / calling?	Wer ist am Apparat?
How can I help you?	Wie kann ich Ihnen helfen?
Can (May) I help you?	Was kann ich für Sie tun?
This is Doris Child, Dr. Brain's secretary.	Hier ist Doris Child, Dr. Brains Sekretärin.
I'm calling on behalf of Dr. Brain.	Ich rufe im Auftrag von Herrn Brain an.

... and goodbye

Thank-you for calling.	Vielen Dank für Ihren Anruf.
Goodbye.	Auf Wiederhören.

Teletiquette: When not to use the company phone

There are certain things that Mr Tickersun should not do over the phone. They are done personally, face to face, so

don't { fire your employees / criticise them / congratulate them / praise them } on the phone

Don't eat, drink or type while you are talking on the phone. The party at the other end of the line might notice it. And don't give the impression that you are overworked and tired.

Teletactics: "Hello" and "goodbye" are not good enough for the company

When *receiving* an in-coming call don't use these words – *unless* you want to *ruin the company's image*. They could mean the beginning and the end of a *business relationship*.
Answer the phone in a warm and *relaxed voice*.
Here are some examples:

receiving	*erhalten*
unless	*es sei denn*
ruin the company's image	*dem Firmenimage schaden*
business relationship	*Geschäftsbeziehung*
relaxed voice	*entspannte Stimme*

This is how most receptionists answer the phone:
"Satco Company, can I help you?"

This telefunction is perfectly alright. But you will *miss the opportunity* of creating the *relationship* to a customer. Here's a telefunction that makes you *appear* more personal.

miss the opportunity	*sich die Gelegenheit entgehen lassen*
relationship	*Beziehung*
appear	*erscheinen lassen*

"Satco Company, Good morning.
Anne Wilder speaking. What can I do for you?"

Give the *callers* the *impression* that they are welcome. On the other hand, you shouldn't overdo it. *Remain natural* and don't act.

Anrufer · Eindruck

bleiben Sie natürlich

The first and often the last impression that a *client* gets of your company is over the phone. It is an *opportunity* to create a customer relationship beyond the reach of your *competitors*. Look at this example:

Kunde

Gelegenheit

Konkurrenten

"Pelc Company, your personal language consultant in Germany.
Rainer Bost speaking. What can I do for you?"

Time for a smile

Not knowing who you are talking to can be dangerous, as this phone story shows:
Tom and Tina Tickersun had been married for twenty years without children. Then one day, the doctor told Tina that she was expecting a baby. Excitedly[1] she rang up Tom in his office. "Tom, just imagine[2], I am pregnant[3]." "That's great," exclaimed Tickersun. After a long silence, then Tom : "I beg your pardon, who is speaking?"

Tina could have avoided[4] this awkward[5] misunderstanding if she had given her name first. Since this is a private call she might have said, "Hello Tom, this is Tina speaking". On the other hand, Mr Tickersun should have asked: "Who is calling?"

1 aufgeregt 2 stell dir vor 3 schwanger 4 vermeiden 5 peinlich

Your Teletrainer

EXERCISE 1

Put the following sentences from a phone call into their chronological order. Give each sentence its correct number.

This is Dr. Brain here.
Can I be of help?
I' d like to speak to Mr Tickersun, please.
Who is calling, please?
MBI, good morning. Doris Child speaking. Can I help you?
I'm afraid Mr Tickersun is at a meeting.

4

EXERCISE 2

Sie sind Tom. Sie rufen Dr. Brian Brain an:

Sagen Sie, wer Sie sind.	*Hello Brian. T... .. Tom .....ing.*
Fragen Sie, ob er etwas Zeit hat.	*I....... if you could .... me a minute.*
Bieten Sie an, zu einer anderen Zeit zurückzurufen.	*Or ..... I call ..... some other time?*
Sagen Sie, daß Sie im Auftrag von Herrn Tickersun anrufen.	*I'm calling .. .. Mr Tickersun, you know.*

EXERCISE 3

Mimi is a German receptionist. Her English is rather strange. Can you correct her mistakes?

Mimi:	*Company Satco. Good day. Where is there?*
Yono:	*This is Yono Onosa from Syno Limited. Could I speak to Mr Knut, please?*
Mimi:	*Sorry, I fear you can him not speak . Mr Knut is not there. He has a bespeaking.*
Yono:	*I'm afraid, the line is bad, I don't quite understand. I'll try again. Goodbye.*
Mimi:	*Please, how you wish. On again hearing. (She hangs up)... Diese Asiaten sollten wirklich etwas für ihr Englisch tun!*

Your Teledoc: Don't panic when the phone rings

Some people *panic* in the lift, others on board a plane, and others panic when the telephone rings. Are you one of those who *dislike* the idea of talking to somebody whose face you can't see? Do you *feel uncomfortable* because you don't know where they're calling from, what their real *voice* might *sound* like, and if his or her words are in harmony with his *body language*?	*in Panik geraten* *nicht mögen* *sich unwohl fühlen* *Stimme · klingen* *Körpersprache*
Well, these are certainly some of the *drawbacks* of the telephone. But be honest with yourself! Would you really prefer a *videophone* in order to be able to watch the person at the other end of the line? Aren't you forgetting that the other person could then watch you, as well. This would be the end of your *privacy.* You couldn't *scratch* your head while talking, nor could you loosen your *tie* or *take off* your jacket on a hot day. So don't panic when the telephone rings. Sit back and *relax*. You are *invisible.*	*Nachteile* *Fernsehtelefon* *Privatsphäre* *kratzen* *Schlips · ausziehen* *sich entspannen* *unsichtbar*

Time for a smile

The phone rang in the maternity ward[1]:
Nurse: St. Joseph's hospital. Nurse[2] Cassandra speaking.
Man: I'm bringing my wife – she's going to have a baby. It's urgent[3].
Nurse: Is this her first baby?
Man: No, no. This is her husband.

1 Entbindungsstation 2 Schwester 3 dringend

This was the past ... *... and this is the future*

The latest word in robot technology

Robotalot Household Robots

Quality and reliability are keywords in our company

How can our little helper change your life? Apart from being reliable, Robby has many functions. He can clean your house, cook, wash the dishes and many other things. Robby's not the cheapest. Quality has its price, but he's worth the investment.

Get him and do yourself good!

MR BRAIN PLACES AN ADVERT

CONTENTS

Our Telestory:	**Mr Brain places an advert**
Telefunctions:	**How to ask for information**
	How to put people through
Your Teletrainer:	**Practise your telefunctions**
Teletiquette:	**Ten Commandments**
Your Teledoc:	**Create your image**
Telejokes:	**Time for a smile**

Time for a smile

Misunderstandings on the phone are often caused by words that sound alike but have a different meaning.

Secretary: Hello Bob. Have you any four-volt, two-watt bulbs[1]?
Storeman: For what?
Secretary: No, two.
Storeman: Two what?
Secretary: Yes, two watt.
Storeman: So what? Well, I'm afraid in that case you have to use our company's order forms[2] ... and add a picture, please.

1 Glühbirne 2 Bestellformular

A Stroke of good luck

Dr. Brian Brain was fired. Then followed a period of *worry* about the future. He had *developed* a *multi-purpose* robot, but couldn't *afford* to perfect it. Then he had a stroke of luck. He came, he saw, he *conquered* – Jacky Ascot, daughter of a millionaire. After four months they were *engaged*. Let's listen into one of their telephone conversations, an almost fatal misunderstanding:
Jacky: I'm calling from the hotel and now that we're engaged, I hope you'll give me a *ring*.
Brian: Yes, of course. What's your number?

Sorge · entwickelt
Vielzweck- · sich leisten können
erobern
verlobt
Ring oder Anruf

Jacky already *possessed* a company called Robotalot which was unfortunately rather *run down*. However, with Jacky's money and his know-how Brain soon built it up, ready to *break into* the market. Now Dr. Brain could develop his robot to "perfection". He *carried on* with the research and a year later it was time to start selling and marketing. He needed a *salesman*. Dr. Brain phoned the newspaper to find out how to *place an advertisement*.

besitzen
heruntergekommen
eindringen
fortfahren
Verkäufer
Inserat aufgeben

Brian Brain places an advert

Clara Late (**L**), Dr.Brain(**B**)

L: Late News, Miss Clara Late speaking. Good afternoon.

B: Hello, my name is Brain. I'd like to *enquire* about the possibility of *placing a job advertisement* in your newspaper.

anfragen
inserieren · Stellenanzeige

L: Excuse me, What did you say your name was? ... The Brian Brain who married Jacky Ascot? How can I be of help?

B: Well, could you tell me what it costs?	
L: Of course, sir. The *advertisement* will cost you £4 per line. You can have a maximum of ten lines per *advert*. The *letter size* is 0.5 cm or 1 cm in *height*.	*Anzeige* · *Anzeige* · *Schriftgröße* · *Höhe*
B: £4 per line?! I *bet* you've got a good business going. Well anyway, I was *wondering* when it would *appear*.	*annehmen* · *sich fragen* · *erscheinen*
L: Job adverts always appear in the Friday *edition*.	*Ausgabe*
B: I'd like to know *whether* I could get a *discount* if I place an advert and keep it in for three weeks.	*ob* · *Rabatt*
L: No, I'm sorry. No *quantity discounts* here! You pay for our quality.	*Mengenrabatt*
B: That's what I like to see – flexibility.	
L: Well sir, as my father always says, we don't need to be flexible. We're the only newspaper in the district. *(to be continued)*	

Time for a smile: Being connected

Absentminded[1] Mr Tickersun had left his shopping bag containing[2] fish, milk and cheese in a train on his way home. The next morning, having realized the loss, he rang up British Rail[3].

Mr Tickersun (**T**), Operator (**O**), Employee (**E**)

O: British Rail, can I help you?

T: Excuse me, madam, I wonder if you could tell me how to get my shopping bag back. I seem to have left it on the Oxford train, but I don't remember ...

O: One moment, please. I'll put you through to the Lost Property Department[4]. *(Music)*

E: Information desk[5]. Can I help you?

1 zerstreut 2 eine Einkaufstasche mit 3 die Britische Bahngesellschaft 4 Fundbüro 5 Auskunft

T: Tickersun here. I was wondering if you could help me. I left my shopping bag on ...

E: I'm afraid you've got the wrong number and the wrong department, sir. It's the Lost Property you want. Hold the line, please. *(Music ... after a minute)*

E: Sorry to keep you waiting, but the line seems to be engaged. I'll try again. Hold on, please. I'm putting you through now. *(Again music is piped into Tickersun's ear; he is getting irritated[1] ... after a while)*

E: Sorry for keeping you waiting, but I'm afraid the line's busy. Will you hold? (*after some minutes*). I'm afraid the line is still engaged. Can you hold? I'll transfer you back to switchboard.

O: British Rail, can I help you?

T: Tickersun. Could you put me through to the Lost Property Department, please? By the way ...

O: Oh, it's you again! One moment please. I'll give you the extension[2]. It's two – double nine – eight. Goodbye.

T: Wait a minute! She's gone! Two – double – ... I'll be damned! (*He dials[3] again*).

E: Thank-you for calling British Rail, Bob Morley speaking. A very good morning, sir. What can we do for you?

T: This is Lost Property spea... Oh no! ... This is Mr Tickersun speaking. There is something I'd like to find out. I'd like to know if somebody has returned my shopping bag which I left yesterday ... in the Lost Prop- ... Good Lord! ... on one of the Oxford trains, of course, and ...

E: Sorry, sir, I' m afraid you've dialled the wrong number... hmm ... and it's almost lunch time, you know. By the way, our trains are only cleaned twice a month[4], you see. So there's no hurry. You'd better call back in a week. British Rail wishes you a very good afternoon. Goodbye.

Absentminded Mr Tickersun forgot about the bag, but was reminded[5] of it a week later by the following advert in the Late News:

Would the gentleman who left a bag containing fish, milk and cheese on the Oxford train please report to[6] British Rail. He can have the train.

1 gereizt 2 Durchwahlnummer 3 wählen 4 zweimal im Monat 5 wurde erinnert 6 sich melden bei

Telefunctions

Trying to get information

I'm calling/ringing to find out about ...	Ich rufe an, um zu erfahren ...
I'd like to enquire about ...	Ich hätte eine Frage zu ...
Could you please explain ... ?	Können Sie mir bitte erklären ...?
I wonder if you could tell me ...?	Könnten Sie mir bitte sagen ...?
I was wondering if you could help me ...	Würden Sie so freundlich sein und mir weiterhelfen ...?
There is something I'd like to find out ...	Ich würde gerne wissen ...

How to connect people

I'll put you through.	Ich verbinde Sie.
I'll transfer you to the right department.	Ich verbinde Sie mit der richtigen Abteilung.
I'll connect you (with ...).	Ich verbinde Sie (mit ...).
I'm passing you on to ...	Ich gebe das Gespräch weiter an ...

How (not) to keep them waiting

I'm afraid the line is engaged/busy.	Die Leitung ist leider belegt.
There's no reply from the extension.	Die Nummer meldet sich nicht.
I'll pass you back to the switchboard.	Ich gebe Sie zurück an die Zentrale.
Can you hold?	Können Sie dranbleiben?
Will you hold?	Wollen Sie warten?
Hold on, please.	Bleiben Sie bitte dran.
Please hold the line.	Bleiben Sie bitte am Apparat.
Would you like to hold on?	Möchten Sie warten?
You dialled the wrong number.	Sie haben sich verwählt.
I'll give you the extension.	Ich gebe Ihnen die Durchwahlnummer.
You'd better call back.	Am besten, Sie rufen zurück.

it's not allowed to give you the ext.

Teletiquette: Ten commandments for receptionists and secretaries

The employees of British Rail obviously know their telefunctions. But what about *etiquette* on the phone? Here are the (first) *ten commandments* for *operators* and *receptionists*:	*Benehmen, Manieren* · *Zehn Gebote · Telefonisten · Empfangspersonal*
1. Don't connect callers *on suspicion*. Don't *waste* their time and money.	*auf Verdacht* · *verschwenden*
2. *Make sure* that they remember numbers and names correctly. Make them *repeat* the information you have given them.	*sichergehen* · *wiederholen*
3. Don't give callers an *extension* without knowing if their contacts are *available*.	*Nummer der Nebenstelle* · *erreichbar*
4. Don't *keep* callers *waiting* when you cannot put them through.	*warten lassen*
5. Don't *pass* them *back* to the *operator*. Connect them personally.	*zurückvermitteln · Vermittlung*
6. Make sure that the *relevant persons* are there. Tell them what the call is about.	*die betreffenden Personen*
7. If it *takes time* to get through to the relevant person, don't park your *callers*; get back to them in *intervals* of 20 seconds and tell them why you have to make them wait.	*Zeit brauchen* · *Anrufer* · *Abstände*
8. *Offer* to *call back*, if you can't put the *caller* through.	*anbieten · zurückrufen* · *Anrufer*
9. Don't put *clients* through without having *apologised* for having kept them waiting.	*Kunden* · *entschuldigen*
10. Thank them for their *patience*.	*Geduld*

Your Teletrainer

EXERCISE 1

Do you remember the verbs?

I'll p . . you t . . . . . .
I'll t . . . . you to
I'll c . . . . . . you w . . .

EXERCISE 2

Put the following sentences from a phone call into their chronological order. Give each sentence its correct number.

Just a moment, please. ....
Excuse me, madam, could you put me through to the Lost Property Department? ....
Britsh Rail, can I help you? ....
I think I'll try again later. When would be the best time to call back? ....
Sorry, the line is engaged. Can you hold or would you like to call again?

EXERCISE 3

Complete the dialogue

A word you might need: call about (anrufen wegen)

Tom Smarty:	*Mrs Brain:*
Good afternoon. I'd like to s.... to Mr Brain.	*I'm sorry. He's still at the factory. Would you like to l... a message?*
Yes please. I' m .... the advert in the Late News. What would be a good time to call back?	*The best time would be after eight o'clock. What did you ..... your name ......?*
Smarty, Tom Smarty.	*Well, Mr Smarty, I'll tell my husband that you ....*
Thank-you, Mrs Brain. Goodbye.	*Goodbye.*

EXERCISE 4

Please complete the dialogue

Words you might need:* (Ausweispapiere) *documents,* (sich erinnern) *remember,* (beschreiben) *describe,* (buchstabieren) *spell

British Rail. .... you?	*Mrs Sills ..... Could you ... me .... to Lost Property?*
.... a moment. I'm c......ing you.	*Thank-you.*
Lost property. ... I .. of ....?	*I'd like .. .. if someone has handed in my handbag.*
Do you remember ..... you lost it?	*In Victoria Station, I think.*
And .... was that?	*Friday evening. At about 9 o'clock. All my documents were in it.*
Documents? In that case I'll have to .... over .. my colleague.	
It's .... for you.	*Thank-you.*
John Smith .... My colleague told me that your handbag is missing. Could you give me some more details?	*Sure, it's a small brown leather handbag.*
What ... you ... your ....?	*Sills, Susan Sills.*
Could you ..... that, please?	*Es Ai double l es, Sills.*
May I ask .... you were born, Mrs Sills?	*I was born on October 20th, 1948.*
You are lucky, Mrs Sills. I've got your handbag right in front of me on my desk.	*Oh great! I'll come right now and collect it.*

DEFUSING[1] THE ANGRY CUSTOMER

CONTENTS

Our Telestory:	**Dr. Brain makes a complaint**
Speech functions:	**The language of complaints**
Teletactics:	**How to handle angry customers**
Your Teletrainer:	**Practise your speech functions**
Your Teledoc:	**Create your image**
More Telejokes:	**There's always time for a smile**

Time for a smile

An elderly lady[2] phones the director of the hotel:
"John Grey speaking. Can I help you?"
"Yes, please. I've a complaint[3] to make. There are two men under my bed. I insist[4] that you come immediately[5] and throw[6] one of them out."

1 entschärfen 2 ältere Dame 3 Reklamation, Beschwerde 4 bestehen (auf) 5 sofort 6 hinauswerfen

Dr. Brian Brain makes a complaint

Dr. Brian Brain is looking for an *efficient* salesperson to sell his *multi-purpose* office robot. So he *placed a job advertisement* in the local paper. When he wanted to see what it looked like but couldn't find it he *furiously* rushed to the phone and called the news paper to *complain*.	*tüchtig* · *Vielzweck-* · *inserieren* · *wütend* · *sich beschweren*
Brian Brain (**B**), Switchboard (**S**), Bob Late, son of the owner of Late News (**L**)	
S: Late News. Good evening. Can I help you?	
B: I hope so. Would you put me through to the *advertising department*, please. I've a *serious complaint* to make.	*Annoncenabteilung* · *ernste Beschwerde*
S: I'm sorry to hear that, sir. I'll *connect* you with Bob Late, from the advertising department. *The phone is ringing for you.*	*verbinden* · *Sie werden verbunden.*
L: Advertising department, Bob Late speaking. Can I help you?	
B: I'd very much like to complain. I placed my advert to *appear* in your Late News on Friday, two weeks ago.	*erscheinen*
L: What is the *reason* for your complaint?	*Grund*
B: The reason is that it wasn't there.	
L: In that case your complaint seems to be more than *justified*. Something has *obviously* gone wrong. We'll *look into* it *immediately*.	*gerechtfertigt* · *offensichtlich* · *untersuchen* · *unverzüglich*
B: Well, that isn't all. When I *finally* saw the ad last Friday already one week *late* it was full of *mistakes*.	*endlich* · *zu spät* · *Fehler*
L: One moment please, Mr Brain. I'm *taking a few notes*. What sort of mistakes?	*einige Notizen machen*
B: My name was *incorrectly* printed.	*falsch*
L: That's a real *nuisance*. I can understand why you are *dissatisfied*.	*Ärgernis* · *unzufrieden*

B: I'm afraid, I can't *accept* that sort of thing. And the advert was for a *"salt man"*!!	*hinnehmen · ak* *Salzmann*
L: Sorry sir, *what on earth* is a salt man?	*was in aller Welt*
B: You may well ask. None of the *applicants* knew either – of the two that *bothered* to reply. *It should have read* "salesman"!!	*Bewerber* *die sich die Mühe machten* *Es hätte lauten sollen*
L: Oh! We owe you more than *an apology*, sir. How can we *make up* for the *inconvenience* we have caused you?	*Entschuldigung* *wiedergutmachen · Unannehmlichkeiten*
B: Well, you could *put* the advert *in* tomorrow, Friday. But properly.	*einschieben*
L: ... and on Saturday as well, Mr Brain, with *no extra charge*, of course.	*ohne Zusatzkosten*
B: That *sounds reasonable*, Mr Late.	*vernünftig klingen*
L: I'm *relieved* that we managed to sort this out, Mr Brain. I *assure* you that this sort of thing won't *happen* again.	*erleichtert* *versichern* *passieren*

Time for a smile

Mrs Brain who was on a cruise[1] on board a luxury liner[2], called the First Officer. "Excuse me, I want to express my dissatisfaction[3]. Last night, while I was undressing[4], a sailor peeped[5] into my cabin." "What do you expect for second class," replied[6] the officer, "the captain?"

1 Kreuzfahrt 2 Luxus-Kreuzfahrtschiff 3 Unzufriedenheit 4 sich ausziehen 5 schauen, kibitzen 6 antworten

Speech functions

The language of complaints	
I've got a serious complaint to make.	Ich habe eine schwerwiegende Reklamation.
I'd very much like to complain.	Ich möchte mich beschweren.
I really want to complain most strongly.	Ich möchte mit allem Nachdruck reklamieren.
I really can't accept this kind of thing again.	Ich kann so etwas einfach nicht noch mal hinnehmen.

What to say to the angry customer	
I'm awfully sorry to hear that.	Das tut mir furchtbar leid.
What is the reason for your complaint?	Was ist der Grund für Ihre Beschwerde?
In this case your complaint seems to be more than justified.	In diesem Fall scheint Ihre Reklamation mehr als gerechtfertigt.
Something has obviously gone wrong.	Da ist offensichtlich etwas schiefgelaufen.
We'll look into it immediately.	Wir werden es sofort überprüfen.
That's a real nuisance.	Das ist wirklich ärgerlich.
I can understand why you are dissatisfied.	Ich kann verstehen, daß Sie unzufrieden sind.
We owe you more than an apology, sir.	Wir schulden Ihnen mehr als nur eine Entschuldigung.
How can we make up for the inconvenience?	Wie können wir die Unannehmlichkeiten wiedergutmachen?
I'm relieved that we managed to sort this out.	Ich bin erleichtert, daß wir das klären konnten.
I assure you that this sort of thing won't happen again.	Ich versichere Ihnen, daß so etwas nicht wieder vorkommt.

Teletactics: How to handle angry customers in five steps

1. Zuhören und sprechen lassen

May I ask what the problem is?	Was haben Sie für ein Problem?
Would you be so kind as to describe your problem?	Würden Sie mir bitte Ihr Problem beschreiben?
Then I can do something to help you.	Dann kann ich etwas unternehmen, um Ihnen zu helfen.

2. "Entschuldigung" nicht vergessen

Let me first apologise for this situation.	Zuerst möchte ich mich dafür entschuldigen.
I'm awfully sorry to hear that.	Das tut mir furchtbar leid.
Please accept our apologies.	Bitte akzeptieren Sie unsere Entschuldigung.
Something has obviously gone wrong.	Da ist offensichtlich etwas schiefgelaufen.

3. Zeigen Sie Mitgefühl

That's really a nuisance.	Das ist wirklich ärgerlich.
I'm sure your complaint is justified.	Ich bin sicher, Ihre Reklamation ist gerechtfertigt.
I can understand why you are dissatisfied.	Ich kann Ihre Unzufriedenheit verstehen.
I can imagine your disappointment.	Ich kann mir Ihre Enttäuschung vorstellen.

4. Zusammenarbeit anbieten

I'll look into it immediately.	Ich werde es sofort überprüfen.
We'll check the problem and call you back immediately.	Wir klären das Problem ab und rufen Sie sofort zurück.
How can we make up for the damage?	Wie können wir den Schaden wiedergutmachen?

5. Finden Sie die Lösung gemeinsam

Thank-you for your suggestions for improving our product.	Vielen Dank für Ihre Verbesserungsvorschläge.
I'm pleased we managed to sort it all out.	Ich freue mich, daß wir die Angelegenheit regeln konnten.

Your Teletrainer

EXERCISE 1: Complete the joke

Bill Carter's farm is only 300 yards away from the new chemical plant. One morning he found one of his prize hens dead in the yard again. He rushed to the phone and got hold of Tim Hart, head of the Public Relations Department:

TH: Oh! It's you again, Mr Carter. What seems to be the . . . . today?

BC: I'm afraid I must . . . . very . . . . . . ly. This is the third time that I've found one of my prize hens lying on its back with all its feathers gone. Could you explain that to me?

TH: Well, Mr Carter, I suppose this hen is dead, too.

EXERCISE 2: The right order

Put the following sentences from a phone call into their chronological order. Give each sentence its correct number.

A: What are you going to do about it, if I may ask?	*7*
B: May I ask what the problem is?	
A: I've got a serious complaint to make. The vacuum cleaner I bought yesterday doesn't work properly.	
B: I' m relieved we managed to sort it all out. Please ask for Miss Roomy. Good-bye.	
A: Well, it doesn't suck in the dust. It blows it out.	
B: Please accept our apology.	
B: I'm awfully sorry to hear that. That's really a nuisance.	
A: That sounds reasonable. I'll be along in an hour. Goodbye.	
B: If you bring the vacuum cleaner, I'll look into it immediately. Of course, we'll pay for the taxi.	
B: Media Center, good morning. What can I do for you?	

EXERCISE 3: How to complain

Ergänzen Sie die folgenden Speech functions mit einem der Ausdrücke: *afraid, make, complain, accept, dissatisfied*

I don't normally . . . . but this is really too much.
I'm afraid I've got to . . . . a serious complaint.
I really can't . . . . . . this kind of thing again.
I'm . . . . . . I can't accept that.
I've been totally . . . . with your customer service so far.

EXERCISE 4: How to react to complaints

Ergänzen Sie die folgenden Speech functions mit einem der Ausdrücke: *explain, ask, owe, check, realise, sort, hear*

May I . . . what the problem is?
I'm awfully sorry to . . . . that.
We . . . . you an apology for the delay.
I . . . . . . that this may put you in a difficult position.
May I . . . . . . the matter from our point of view?
We'll . . . . . the problem and call you back immediately.
I'm sure we can . . . . this out.

EXERCISE 5: Translate

A: Spreche ich mit dem Kundendienst? Ich habe eine Reklamation. Wir haben Schreibmaschinenpapier[1] bestellt. Das war vor einem Monat. Es ist noch nicht eingetroffen.

B: Da ist offensichtlich etwas schiefgelaufen. Wir überprüfen das und rufen Sie sofort zurück.

---

1 typing paper

Your Teledoc: Create your image

Have you ever tried to see how close you can get to a person? Try it; say a few nice words to a colleague, get closer and closer and you will realise that he or she will *be embarrassed* and will instinctively step back as soon as you get nearer than 20 centimetres to his or her face.	*peinlich berührt sein*
On the telephone, however, you are directly at a person's ear without making him *feel uncomfortable*. Good communicators know how to *exploit* this *opportunity*. They do things on the phone which are impossible in a face to face situation. An *elderly* small and tired-looking salesman can create a youthful and dynamic image of himself only by using the right words and *striking the right tone*. Find the right words, strike the right tone and the telephone becomes a *powerful* instrument in business.	*sich unwohl fühlen* *ausnutzen · Gelegenheit* *älterer* *den richtigen Ton finden* *mächtig*
Striking the right tone – I know that's easier said than done. However, you will find some *good pieces of advice* in our extra-reading texts about etiquette on the phone.	*gute Ratschläge*

Time for smile

A famous French film producer, Jean Yves Goday, went to Hollywood to shoot a western[1] for which he needed an enormous herd of young bulls[2]. He was advised[3] to contact one of the big Texan ranchers. He phoned the first he found in the yellow pages[4]:
"Is that Mr Adams?" "Speaking." "It's Goday, the film director. I hope I'm not disturbing you, Mr Adams." "Not at all. How can I help you?"
"Mr Adams, we've got a problem. Would it be possible at all to put a herd of 30,000 bulls on hoof[5] within four days?"
"No problem. Do you want black, white or brown bulls?"

1 einen Western drehen 2 eine Herde junger Bullen 3 man riet ihm 4 Branchenverzeichnis
5 auf die Beine (Hufe) bringen

SUGGESTIONS AND GOOD ADVICE

CONTENTS

Our Telestory :	**Why don't you apply for the job?**
Telefunctions:	**The language of private calls**
Speech functions:	**Suggestions and good advice**
Your Teletrainer:	**Let's practise them**
Your Teledoc:	**Body language on the phone?**
Our Telejokes:	**Time for a smile**

Time for a smile

In a Berlin newspaper actor Harry Junky reads news about his early death. He immediately telephones his friend, Tommy Godjester:

Harry: Have you read this? It says I'm dead.

Tommy: Of course I have. Where are you phoning from?

Why don't you apply for the job?

As we learned in the *previous* chapter, Dr. Brain, now boss of his own robot *manufacturing company*, had placed advertisements in the newspaper for a salesperson to sell the super robot to *various sectors* of industry. Fussy Pot, girlfriend of Andrew Goodman, sees the *ad* and *immediately* phones Andrew. He is a rather *lazy* sort of person, but quite clever.

Fussy (**F**), Andrew (**A**)

F: Hi, Andrew, it's me Fussy.
A: Oh really, how are things?
F: I can't *complain*. You *sound* as if you weren't expecting me to phone. Were you *expecting* somebody else?
A: Me? No! I'm just *taking it easy*. I'm resting a bit. *Getting away* from the world.
F: Well, if you take my *advice*, you'll start looking around for a good job. Look, I've just seen an advert in the paper for a robot salesman. And I *reckon* you should go for it.
A: A what salesman, did you say?
F: Robots! They want you to sell *multi-purpose robots*, to do things in the home, in offices or hospitals and so on. Why don't you *apply* for the job?
A: It might be *something different for a change*. Can you give me a few details?
F: There's not a lot of information here but it says *you are expected* to work hard and you'll have about £50,000 a year, six weeks holiday and you'll need a short training.
A: Work hard? *Where's the company located?* What else would they expect me to do?
F: You'd have to *travel* a lot and ... Listen,

vorangehend
Fabrik
verschiedene Industriezweige · *Anzeige* · *sofort*
faul
sich beklagen · *klingen*
erwarten
ausspannen
entfliehen
Rat
meinen
Vielzweckroboter
sich bewerben
zur Abwechslung was anderes
man erwartet von dir
Wo ist/sitzt die Firma?
reisen

wouldn't it be a good idea, if you had a look at the ad yourself?	
A: Okay. Can you bring it *round to my place*? I'll	*zu mir nach Hause*
look it *over*. So long.	*ansehen*
F: I'll be with you in a minute. *Cheers.*	*tschüs*

Telefunctions: Private calls

Fussy and Andrew used telefunctions typical for informal calls. Here are some more.

1. You start with "Hello ..."	
This is Brain speaking.	Mein Name ist Brain.
Tickersun speaking (privat).	Tickersun am Apparat.
It's Tom here.	Hier ist Tom.
Hi, Paul.	Hallo Paul.
It's me, Fuzzy.	Ich bin's, Fuzzy.
Is Andrew in?	Ist Andrew da?
I'll see if he's in.	Ich sehe nach, ob er da ist.

2. You make a few "polite noises"	
I'm pleased to get hold of you.	Wie schön, daß ich dich erreiche.
I haven't heard from you for ages.	Habe eine Ewigkeit nichts mehr von dir gehört.
How has life been treating you?	Wie ist es dir so ergangen?
How are you keeping?	Wie geht es dir ?
How are you doing?	Wie geht's dir so?
How are things?	Wie geht's? Wie läuft's bei dir?
Nice to speak to you.	Nett, mit Ihnen zu sprechen.
It's been nice to hear from you.	Nett, von Ihnen zu hören.

3. Finally you say "Goodbye"	
Keep in touch!	Laß wieder von dir hören.
Take care!	Mach's gut. Paß auf dich auf.
See you!	Bis später.
So long!	Bis zum nächsten Mal.
Cheers!	Tschüs. / Danke schön.

Speech functions: Suggestions and good advice

In the above dialogue Fussy wants her friend to apply for a job. Instead of imperatives (do this! do that!) she formulated her wishes as suggestions (Vorschläge).

I suggest looking the ad over.	Ich schlage vor, wir gehen die Anzeige einmal durch.
I suggest that you apply for the job.	Ich schlage vor, daß du dich um die Stelle bewirbst.
If you take my advice ...	Wenn ich dir einen Rat geben darf ...
I reckon you should ...	Ich meine, du solltest ...
I think it would be better if ...	Ich glaube, es wäre besser, wenn ...
Wouldn't it be a good idea if ...?	Wäre es nicht besser, wenn ...?
Have you ever thought of ...?	Hast du je daran gedacht zu ...?
Why not apply now?	Warum bewirbst du dich nicht gleich?
Why don't you ring them up now?	Warum rufst du sie nicht gleich jetzt an?
I advise you to take the job.	Ich rate dir, die Stelle anzunehmen.
Don't you think we should consider it?	Meinst du nicht, wir sollten uns das überlegen?
I think we should consider it.	Ich meine, wir sollten es in Betracht ziehen.
I can recommend it.	Ich kann es empfehlen.

ATTENTION: I suggest doing or I suggest (that) you do

1. *I suggest **buying** a new car:*	der Sprecher bezieht sich in den Vorschlag mit ein
2. *I suggest **that you buy** a car:*	der Sprecher nennt die Adressaten seines Vorschlags

Your Teletrainer: Suggestions and private calls

EXERCISE 1:

Choose the function that best completes the sentence

1a I suggest that
1b I suggest to ▶ *you apply for the job immediately.*
1c I suggest

2a I suggest that
2b I suggest to ▶ *asking for more information first.*
2c I suggest

3a Wouldn't it be a good idea
3b Wouldn't it be a good idea to ▶ *you phoned the company now?*
3c Wouldn't it be a good idea if

4a Wouldn't it be a good idea
4b Wouldn't it be a good idea to ▶ *ask for an interview?*
4c Wouldn't it be a good idea if

5a Why don't we
5b Why not ▶ *took a look at other ads?*
5c What if we

Schreiben Sie den richtigen Buchstaben hinter die Zahl, und vergleichen Sie anschließend Ihre Lösung mit dem Schlüssel zu den Übungen.

1 .... 2 .... 3 .... 4 .... 5 ....

EXERCISE 2: Complete the joke

The wife of a rich American banker received[1] the following phone call from a gang who had kidnapped her husband. "We demand one million dollars as a ransom[2] for your husband. We . . . . . . [3] you to pay or you'll never see him again." After a moment's thought the woman replied[4]: "Well, may I . . . . a compromise? You will get the money on the condition[5] that you keep my husband."

1 erhalten 2 Lösegeld 3 raten 4 antworten 5 Bedingung

EXERCISE 3: A private call. Complete our telestory

Fred Niemec is unemployed. After several months of doing nothing and in addition getting problems with his girlfriend, he decided to try to get a job. Susan saw the advert and thought it might be a good idea if he tried his hand as a salesman.

S: Is that you, Tony? . . . . Susan here.
T: Hello Susan, ... you keeping?
S: The usual stress. Is Fred . . ? I've been trying . . . . . hold . . him for the last few days. It's urgent.
T: Just a moment. . ' . . . . . if he's . . . (after a while) He' s coming. I had to wake him up. Well, Susan, it's been nice h . . . . . g from you. K . . . . . touch.
F: Hello, Susan. Haven't . . . . . from you . . . ages. . . . . . . things?
S: Fine, thank you. I've been trying . . . . . in t . . . h . . . . you for quite a while. Why didn't you . . . . back? Didn't you get my message? Listen, I think I've found just the right job for you.
F: A job! Not again. You know I haven't recovered from the last one you found me.
S: It's always the same with you. Why not earn some money for a change? I'll be with you in a minute. I suggest you have a look over the advert. So . . . . .

EXERCISE 4: Do you remember these polite noises?

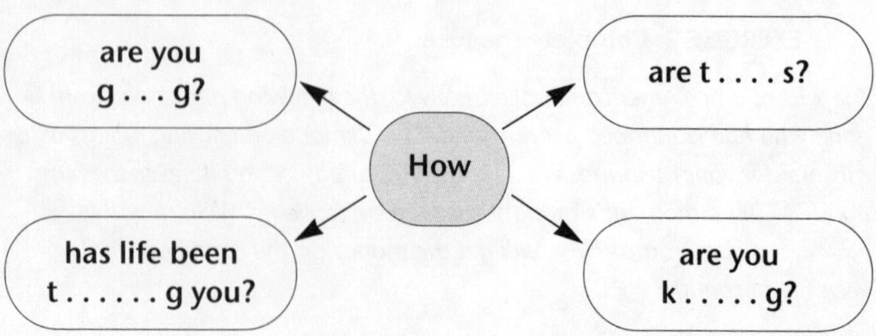

Your Teledoc: Body language on the phone?

Words aren't everything in a conversation. Only about 20 per cent of your *message* is *conveyed* by your words and about 40 per cent by your body language. Another 40 per cent of what you want to tell a person is *expressed* by	*Botschaft · mitteilen* *ausdrücken*
• *tone*	*Tonfall*
• *volume*	*Lautstärke*
• *speed*	*Geschwindigkeit*
• *intonation*	*Intonation*
It is *obvious* that the way we speak on the phone is most important, because we cannot see each other. Speak in a natural tone, a *relaxed voice.* Here is some *advice*:	*offensichtlich* *entspannt* *Stimme · Rat*
1. *Posture influences* the way you speak. Sit *upright* throughout the conversation. *Slumping* over the phone makes your voice sound older and less dynamic.	*Haltung · beeinflussen* *gerade* *zusammensacken*
2. *Take a deep breath* before the other person answers the phone.	*tief einatmen*
3. Sit relaxed and you'll *sound* like it.	*klingen*
4. Your smile will be heard on the other end of the line. Smile and it'll become part of what you are going to say.	
5. Stand up if you want to sound *assertive.*	*bestimmt, selbstsicher*

Tin Lizzy, Ltd

opens up the New Age

Do you sometimes feel you're wasting your time doing boring everyday tasks?
They cost you time, and time is money.

Now here we have the answer:

Tin Lizzy is everybody's helper. He (or she – a question of taste and design) works both at home and in your office, cleans, cooks, carries, feeds the cat and walks the dog.

Tin Lizzy is cheap but still has a lot of functions, and he /she is guaranteed for half a year.

Help yourself!
Do it now! Invest in Tin Lizzy.

SCREENING OFF THE BOSS

CONTENTS

Our Telestory:	Trying to get in touch with the boss
Telefunctions:	Identifying and screening
Teletactics:	Screening strategies
Your Teletrainer:	Test your telefunctions
Teletiquette:	If you can't put them through
More Telejokes:	Time for a smile

Time for a smile: Murphy's telephone laws

1. The telephone will ring when you are outside the door, fumbling[1] for your keys.
2. You will reach it just in time to hear the click of the caller hanging up.
3. When you dial the wrong number, you never get a busy signal[2].

Arthur Bloch

1 suchen, fummeln 2 Besetztzeichen

Trying to get in touch with the boss (1)

Both Fussy and Susan finally get Andrew and Fred to apply for the job. Unfortunately it's a busy day at Robotalot. Dr. Brain has told the receptionist not to put any calls through. Fred makes his first *attempt* to get more information about the job. He decides to use the direct method and get in touch with the boss himself. — *Versuch*

Fred Niemec (**F**), Receptionist (**R**)

R: Hello, Robotalot, Jane Simpson speaking. Can I help you?

F: I hope you can. *In fact* that's why I'm phoning. — *genau gesagt*

R: Well, who would you like to speak to?

F: I don't really know *actually*. Well, if I knew I'd tell you his name. — *eigentlich*

R: So what's the *reason* for your call, sir? — *Grund*

F: I saw an ad in the paper for a job.

R: What sort of *position* was that, sir? — *Stelle*

F: Not quite sure. I think it was a salesman or something ... selling computers, I think. Something *new-fangled* anyway. *Doesn't really matter.* If you can sell one thing you can sell them all. — *Neumodisches · ist im Grunde auch egal*

R: May I have your name, please? *I'm not to* put through any unidentified persons. — *ich darf / soll nicht*

F: Niemec, Fred Niemec.

R: Well, Mr Niemec. I'll put you through to Dr. Brain's secretary. Hold the line please.

F: Well, *I would have preferred* to *have a word with* the boss, actually. — *mir wäre es lieber · sprechen mit*

R: The director is *busy* at present. *Since* we have placed a *series* of job advertisements in *various* papers, you'd better check what *post* you are applying for ... — *beschäftigt · da, weil · Reihe · verschiedene · Stelle*

Here we must leave Fred Niemec, but if you are interested in the end of this go to Chapter 7.

Trying to get in touch with the boss (2)

Now let us see if the second applicant, Andrew Goodman (**A**), is luckier.	
R: Robotalot, Jane Simpson speaking.	
A: Andrew Goodman here. Nice to speak to you, Miss Simpson. Could you put me through to the person who *runs* your company?	*leiten*
R: I beg your pardon, I didn't *catch* your name.	*hier: verstehen*
A: Goodman, as in a "good man". Ha ha, just a little joke. Could I speak to the director?	
R: May I ask the *purpose* of your call, Mr Goodman?	*Zweck*
A: *It's in connetion* with the advertisement in Late News. I want to *apply* for the job.	*es handelt sich um* / *bewerben*
R: Just hold the line a moment, please. I'll *check* if he can *take* your call.	*nachsehen* / *entgegennehmen*
While Andrew is listening to some music, the receptionist calls Mr Brain's secretary, Wendy (**W**)	
R: Hi, Wendy. It's Jane speaking. I've got a Mr Goodman on the phone who is very *keen on* speaking to the boss. It's about the advert for a salesman. Shall we put him through?	*erpicht auf*
W: Mr Brain *left strict instructions* that he was not to *be disturbed*. I can't take the call, either. I've got a visitor from France here. Tell him to send us a written *application.*	*strenge Anweisung geben* / *gestört werden* / *Bewerbung*
R: Are you still there, Mr Goodman?	
C: Yes, Miss Simpson, and I cannot tell you how much I've *enjoyed* the music. By the way, my friends call me Andrew.	*genießen*
R: Well, Mr Andrew Goodman, I'm told Dr. Brain is *out on business* at the moment. Why don't you apply for the job in writing like the other *applicants?*	*geschäftlich unterwegs* / *Bewerber*
A: Ehrr ... Goodbye ... Oh ... just a moment ... Why did she *hang up* on me like that?	*auflegen*

Telefunctions: Identifying and screening

How to identify the caller	**Den Anrufer identifizieren**
May I have your name, please?	Dürfte ich Sie um Ihren Namen bitten?
Sorry, I didn't catch your name.	Entschuldigen Sie, ich habe Ihren Namen nicht verstanden.
Could I ask your name, please?	Darf ich Ihren Namen erfahren?
May I ask who is calling?	Darf ich um Ihren Namen bitten?
Who shall I say is calling?	Wen darf ich bitte melden?

Why are they calling?	**Der Grund des Anrufs**
What's the reason for your call?	Was ist der Grund Ihres Anrufs?
May I ask for the purpose of your call?	Darf ich nach dem Zweck Ihres Anrufs fragen?
What's it in connection with?	Um was geht es, bitte?
Who would you like to speak to?	Wen möchten Sie sprechen?
I'm not to put through any unidentified persons.	Ich darf keine anonymen Anrufer verbinden.

How to excuse the boss	**Wie man den Chef entschuldigt**
I'm afraid he's very busy at present.	Ich fürchte, er ist gerade sehr beschäftigt.
He left strict instructions that he was not to be disturbed.	Er hat strenge Anweisung gegeben, nicht gestört zu werden.
I'll check if he can take the call.	Ich frage nach, ob er den Anruf entgegennehmen kann.
He is out on business at the moment.	Er ist gerade geschäftlich unterwegs.
I suggest you try again tomorrow.	Ich schlage vor, Sie versuchen es morgen noch einmal.
Could his secretary help you?	Könnte Ihnen vielleicht seine Sekretärin weiterhelfen?

In our Glossary (14, 16 and 27) you will find more telefunctions about identifying callers, asking the purpose of a call and excusing the boss. Please look them up; you will need them for the exercises.

Teletactics: Screening strategies

1. Managers have one problem *in common*: they *lose* a lot of time on the phone – and time is money. It's their secretaries' job to take care that this time is not *wasted*. They *screen* their bosses from *unnecessary* incoming phone calls. Most of them follow this strategy:	*gemeinsam* *verlieren* *verschwendet* *abschirmen · unnötig*
2. They ask	
a) the *caller's* name,	*Anrufer*
b) where he or she is calling from and	
c) what the *purpose of the call* is.	*Zweck des Anrufs*
3. Then they *decide* if they should	*entscheiden*
a) *deal with* the caller themselves,	*übernehmen*
b) *transfer* the caller to another department,	*weiterverbinden*
c) put the caller through to their boss.	
4. They *distinguish* three different types of callers:	*unterscheiden*
A) important callers the boss wants to talk to: those who *place orders*, those who have the power to ruin the company or those who are a *valuable source* of information. They are put through *immediately*.	*Bestellungen aufgeben* *wertvolle Quelle* *sofort*
B) callers who the secretary is not *able to place*. The secretary is not sure whether to screen the boss or put them through. *Since* they may be important, a return call is *promised*.	*einordnen können* *da, weil* *versprechen*
C) unimportant callers, salesmen for example. Secretaries have *instructions* not to put them through.	*Anweisung*
5. For each of these three types of callers the secretary has a different strategy.	
a) What might the secretary say to type A,	

the important caller, if he/she can't connect him because the boss is at a meeting?
"Good morning, Mr Knot. *Unfortunately* Dr. Brain is at a meeting. He told me to *arrange a return call* with you. When would be a good time for him to call you back?"

b) What might the secretary say to type B, the *unknown* caller?
"Mr Brain is not *available* at the moment. Can I help you? May I ask *the purpose* of your call? Mr Brain will call you back *as soon as possible.*"

c) What will she always say to type C, the salesman who offers computers?
"I *believe* that your computers are high quality, but we are *fully satisfied* with our present supplier. And my boss has given *strict instructions* not to put through any *sales offers.*"

You see, it is not easy to get past a *well-trained* receptionist or an *efficient* secretary. Our applicants have to learn this lesson.

leider
einen Rückruf vereinbaren
unbekannt
erreichbar
Zweck
so bald wie möglich
glauben
völlig zufrieden
strenge Anweisungen
Verkaufsangebote
gut ausgebildet
tüchtig

Your Teletrainer

EXERCISE 1

Fred Niemec has made six strategic mistakes in trying to get through to the boss. Can you find out which? How many mistakes did Andrew make?

EXERCISE 2: Are you flexible?

have
May I . . . . your name, please?

reason for
What's the . . . . your call?

EXERCISE 3: The Receptionists' hitlist of excuses

Here are nine frequently used excuses if the boss can't take a call. Can you complete them?

I'm afraid Mr Brain is not a . . . .able at the moment.
I'm sorry, but Mr Brain is on h . . . . . . this week.
I'm afraid she is o . . o . the office this week.
Mr Brain is away . . b . . . . . s s .
I'm sorry, Mr Brain is at a m . . . ing .
He left strict instructions not to be d . . . . d .
He's in the middle of an i . . . . w .
He has got an important v . . . . . r .
Dr. Brain is very . . . y at the moment.

EXERCISE 4: Translate the dialogue between secretary (S) and client (C)

S: Schneider, IP Computers. Guten Tag.	
C: Guten Tag. Verbinden Sie mich bitte mit dem *Leiter des Kundendiensts.*	*head of customer service*
S: Wie war bitte Ihr Name?	
C: Anton Sparbier. Ich bin ein *Stammkunde.*	*regular client*
S: Um was handelt es sich bitte?	
C: Ich möchte Sie auf einen *Fehler* in einem Ihrer neuen *Modelle* hinweisen.	*defect* *model*
S: Einen Moment, ich verbinde.	

Exercise 5: The telephone rings – what do you say

1. *first, after having lifted the receiver?*
   Good morning. ....you?

2. *if you don't know why a caller is calling?*
   What ....with?

3. *if you don't understand the caller's name?*
   Sorry, I ....

4. *if you aren't sure whether your boss will take the call?*
   I'll ....the call.

EXERCISE 6: Complete the joke

The telephone rings. Dr. Brian Brain's secretary lifts the receiver[1].

Sec: It's your wife, Dr. Brain. Are you going to t . . e the c . . l[2]?

Brain: Oh no, not now. Tell her that I've got a v . . . . . r and that I'll be home late from the office because of an unexpected[3] conference. (smiling) You know why, don't you?

The secretary does as she is told and hangs up[4].

Brain: How did my wife react? Was she very angry?

Sec: Not at all[5]. She only wanted to know if she could absolutely rely[6] on your coming home late.

Teletiquette: If you can't put them through

Sales representatives who have to make a lot of	*Vertreter*
phone calls *are used to* not being put through	*daran gewöhnt sein*
to an *executive*. In all other cases you should:	*leitender Angestellter*
1. ask if you can *take a message*	*etwas ausrichten*
2. arrange a *mutually convenient* time for the caller to call again,	*eine für beide passende Zeit*
3. or, *in case of* an important customer, offer to make a return call. Ask him when it	*im Falle von*
would be convenient for him to *take* the call.	*entgegennehmen*

Time for a smile

It was two o'clock in the morning when Susan phoned Fred Niemec. The phone rang for half an hour before it was picked up and Fred's sleepy voice said, "Hello". "Sorry to get you out of bed at this time of night", said Susan. "That's all right," said Fred, "I had to get up anyway to answer the phone."

1 den Hörer abnehmen 2 den Anruf entgegennehmen 3 unerwartet 4 auflegen 5 keineswegs 6 sich verlassen auf

GETTING AROUND RECEPTIONISTS AND SECRETARIES

CONTENTS

Our Telestory:	**Back to square one**
Telefunctions :	**Getting a person's name**
Teletactics:	**Step by step to the managing director**
Your Teletrainer:	**German English**

Time for a smile

Boss: If Mr Walker calls before I return, tell him to call again at 5 o'clock.

Secretary: OK boss, but what shall I tell if him if he doesn't call?

Back to square one

Andrew got it all wrong in the last chapter and that was a *blow* to him. So he bought a book about how to phone effectively and studied the tactics *recommended* in the chapter "How to Get Around Receptionists and Secretaries" and tried again. Fortunately the receptionist at Robotalot didn't *remember* Andrew's first call:

Receptionist (**R**), Andrew (**A**)

R: Robotalot, Good afternoon. Can I be of help?

A: I hope you can. This is Andrew Goodman speaking. Andrew Goodman, the *robotics consultant.* I'm sure *we've met before.* Anyway this time it's me who's got a problem. I wonder if you can help me. I really *need* to speak to the director, *if I may*. It's a technical subject. It's Mr ... Hmm, it's no good. *It's slipped my mind.*

R: I know. I've a *bad memory for names*, too. You mean Dr. Brain.

A: Yes, Brain. John Brain, of course.

R: No, it's Brian Brain, actually.

A: You've been most helpful. And you've a lovely *voice* on the phone. I'll *mention* that to Mr Brain. By the way, what's your name?

R: Jane Simpson. And thanks for calling.

A: Oh, *I don't want to be a nuisance*, Mrs Simpson, but I've just one more question. Does Dr. Brain come early or *stay late*? You must know better than anyone else. When would it be a good time *to get hold of* him?

R: Dr. Brain is always the first to arrive and *the last to go*. I'm sorry, but I have to end this call, there are lots of other callers *on the line* ...

von vorne anfangen
Schlag
empfohlen
erinnern
Roboterexperte
wir kennen uns
muß
wenn ich darf
er ist mir entfallen
ein schlechtes Namensgedächtnis
Stimme · erwähnen
ich will nicht aufdringlich sein
lange bleiben
erreichen
der letzte, der geht
in der Leitung

Telefunctions

Getting a person's name from the receptionist	
I wonder if you can help me?	Ob Sie mir wohl weiterhelfen könnten?
I really need to speak to X.	Ich muß dringend mit X sprechen.
Please put me through to ...	Verbinden Sie mich bitte mit ...
His name has slipped my mind.	Sein Name ist mir entfallen.
I've a bad memory for names.	Ich habe ein schlechtes Namensgedächtnis.
You wouldn't happen to know his first name?	Sie wissen nicht zufällig seinen Vornamen?
I want to send your buyer a few documents, but I don't know his or her name. Who would that be, please?	Ich möchte Ihrem Einkäufer gerne ein paar Unterlagen schicken, aber ich weiß seinen Namen nicht. Wer könnte das wohl sein?
Unfortunately I've misplaced his business card. Could you let me have his name, please?	Leider habe ich seine Visitenkarte verlegt. Könnten Sie mir bitte seinen Namen geben?

You have sent your brochures – you'll be able to answer the secretary's questions	
Will Mr Brain know why you're calling?	Weiß Herr Brain, warum Sie anrufen?
Will he know who you are?	Weiß er, wer Sie sind?
It's about the documents I sent him.	Es geht um die Unterlagen, die ich ihm zugesandt habe.

Don't expect to be put through immediately	
I'll check where he is.	Ich sehe nach, wo er ist.
I've been told he's out today.	Ich höre, daß er heute außer Hause ist.

How to end the call	
Thanks a lot.	Vielen Dank.
You've been most helpful.	Sie haben mir sehr geholfen.
I'll mention that to Mr Brain.	Ich werde das Herrn Brain gegenüber erwähnen.
You're welcome!	Gern geschehen.

Teletactics: Step by step to the managing director

RULE ONE: Don't ask to be put through to the director

Getting an important person's name and getting through to him is not always as easy as it *sounds*. There is the receptionist or the secretary whose task it is to *screen* the boss from you and your *competitors*. Don't ask to be put through "to the person who *runs the purchasing department*". The receptionist would *immediately* know that you are type C (see page 48), the "unwanted" *sales person*. You would only be put through the following ritual:

klingen
abschirmen
Konkurrenten
leiten · *Einkaufsabteilung*
sofort
Verkäufer

You: I want to speak to the managing director.
Rec.: Will he know who you are and why you are calling?
You: My name is Ronny Smarty. I've an interesting *range* of *copiers* to offer your company.
Rec.: I'll just check where he is. Please hold the line.

(Some *music* would be *piped into your ears* and then:)

Rec.: Hello? I'm sorry. I've *just been told* he's out today.

Palette · *Kopierer*
mit Musik berieselt werden
Wie ich höre

RULE TWO: Don't sell products – offer information

Don't *give the impression* that you want to sell	*Eindruck machen*
anything or to *waste* anybody's time with *sales*	*verschwenden · Verkaufs-*
talk. Receptionists are told not to put through	*gespräch*
unknown sales *representatives*. But they are not	*unbekannt · Vertreter*
trained to *distinguish* between "important"	*unterscheiden*
and "unwanted" information.	
The following call is already an *improvement*:	*Verbesserung*
Rec.: Satco, Jane Smith speaking. Good morning, how can I help you?	
You: This is Ronny Smarty speaking from Xorex Copiers. I'd like to send the *person in charge of the purchasing department* a	*Leiter der Einkaufsabteilung*
few *brochures*, but I don't know his name. Who may that be, please?	*Prospekte*
Rec.: That will be Mr Knot.	
You: Thank you very much. Oh, *by the way*,	*übrigens*
you wouldn't *happen to know* his first name?	*zufällig wissen*
Rec.: It's Robert, Robert Knot.	
You: Thanks a lot. *You've been most helpful.*	*Sie haben mir sehr geholfen*
Rec.: *You're welcome*. Goodbye.	*Keine Ursache*
The next time, you can ask to be put through	
to Mr Knot or his secretary directly. *In the*	*Inzwischen*
meantime Mr Knot will have *received* your brochures. This will be important for your next call.	*erhalten*

RULE THREE: Don't be a stranger – "know" the person you want

Honesty is a good *policy*, but sometimes you have to *fall back* on a *white lie*.

Ehrlichkeit · Strategie
zurückgreifen · Notlüge

Example 1

You: Good afternoon. This is Ronny Smarty speaking. I've got a problem and I wonder if you can help me. I'd like to send the person *in charge* of the purchasing department a few brochures, but I've *misplaced* his/ her *business card*.

verantwortlich für
verlegen
Visitenkarte

Example 2

You: I met your head buyer *the other day* and he asked me to send him our *quotations* for photocopiers. *Unfortunately* I've a bad *memory* for names. I wonder if you can help me?

Rec.: Yes, of course. His name is Knot, Robert Knot.

You: Thank-you very much. You've been most helpful. *By the way*, what's your name?

Rec.: Jane Smith.

neulich
Angebote
leider
Gedächtnis
übrigens

Don't forget to ask the receptionist's name. You will use it when you make your second call. And send Mr Robert Knot your *brochures* before you *take the next step* after a couple of days.

Kataloge · den nächsten Schritt tun

RULE FOUR: Name-dropping

Now you have got the name of both the manager and the receptionist, and you will use them *to your advantage*. You will no longer *sound* like an unwanted or unknown person. And you have a *pretext* to call and you can *refer* to the brochures which *might* already be in the hands of Mr Knot.

zu Ihrem Vorteil
klingen
Vorwand · sich beziehen
könnten

Achieving your aim — *Ihr Ziel erreichen*

You: Good morning, Mrs Smith. This is Ronny Smarty from Xorex. Could you put me through to Robert Knot, please?
Rec.: Will Mr Knot know the reason for your call?
You: It's about the *documents* we sent him last week. — *Unterlagen*
Rec.: Hold the line, please. I'm putting you through.

Do's and Don'ts in a nutshell

- Don't ask to be put through the first time.
- Don't tell them that you have a product to sell.
- Don't sound like a stranger.

First call:

- Get the name from the receptionist.
- "Know" the person you want to contact.
- Offer information instead of products.
- Tell them that he or she is expecting information from you.
- Ask the receptionist's name.

Second call:

- Send your brochures before you make the second call.
- Ask to be put through to Mr Brain.
- Tell the secretary you are calling about the documents you sent him.
- Tell her it is about a highly technical or financial subject.

Your Teletrainer

EXERCISE 1: German English

Mimi übersetzt alles wortwörtlich ins Englische. Das geht natürlich nur in den seltensten Fällen gut. Korrigieren Sie Mimi (Lösungen siehe Schlüssel).

Receptionist (**R**), Mimi (**M**)

R: *Robotalot. Can I help you?*
M: *Yes, that can you. I want your boss speak, Mister äh ... Oh! Now is his name me off fallen.*
R: *I beg your pardon?*
M: *No, Pardon was not his name. Wait you ... I remember me: his forname is Andrew. I have him in Paris met on a computer mess.*
R: *Excuse me, but where are you calling from?*
M: *Calling ? Ach so! I call out Germany.*
R: *Germany? My colleague speaks German. If you give me your telephone number, she will call you back.*
M: *That is a good idea. Mine number is 116671. Thank very. You are very helprich.*

By the way: eine Messe is a trade fair, at church it's mass, and mess means chaos.

EXERCISE 2: Keyword exercise

Keyword	*Do you remember the telefunction?*
assistance	*Can I be of assistance?*
name /slipped	
memory /name	
need/ Mr Brain	
told / out	
helpful	
welcome	

THROUGH TO THE BOSS

CONTENTS

Our Telestory:	The appointment
	Through to the boss
Telefunctions:	A revision
Speech functions:	Describing the way
Your Teletrainer:	Finding the way
Teletactics:	Avoiding rush hours and secretaries
	Telephone marketing
Some Telejokes:	Time for a smile

Time for a smile

A rich banker who had made a fortune[1] at the stock exchange[2] phoned his new mistress[3]:
"Darling, I sent you a birthday present: a Picasso and a Ferrari. Did you get them alright?"
"Yes darling, they are wonderful. But could you please tell me which is the Picasso and which is the Ferrari?"

1 Vermögen 2 Börse 3 Geliebte

The appointment

In the *meantime* Fred Niemec continues his rather wishy-washy discussion (see page 44) with the receptionist. She is beginning to *lose patience.*	*Inzwischen* · *Geduld verlieren*
Receptionist (**R**), Fred Niemec (**F**), Carol Williams (**C**)	
R: ... as I said I'm sorry but Dr. Brain is *extremely* busy *at present.* If you like I'll put you through to the *personnel department.*	*äußerst* · *im Augenblick* · *Personalabteilung*
F: Well, is there *somebody in authority* I can talk to?	*jd., der kompetent ist*
R: Yes, of course, I'll connect you with Dr. Halfar. *Putting you through now.*	*Ich verbinde*
C: Mr Halfar's *office.* Carol Williams speaking.	*Büro*
R: There's a Mr Niemec for Mr Halfar on the phone. Shall I transfer the call to your desk?	
C: Thanks Susan. I'll take the call. ... Carol Williams speaking. Good afternoon. Can I be of *assistance?*	*Hilfe, Beistand*
F: Well, I was expecting to *be connected with* Dr. Halfar.	*verbunden werden*
C: I'm afraid, Mr Halfar is not available. Can I take a message?	
F: I'm phoning about the *post you advertised.*	*die annoncierte Stelle*
C: The *sales position?*	*Verkäuferstelle*
F: Yes, *I guess* that's it. Could you give me a few details about it?	*ich glaube*
C: I can do better than that. I can invite you for a first interview. We're starting interviews tomorrow. We could just *fit* you *in.*	*einplanen*
F: Oh, I hadn't *expected* to have to come so quickly. Can you *fax* me a *map* of how to get there?	*erwarten* · *zufaxen* · *Plan*
C: Not necessary! You just go out of the *railway station* ...	*Bahnhof*

F: Just a minute. I'm coming *by car.*	*mit dem Auto*
C: *In that case* you drive off the *motorway* at the Nottingham sign, turn second right, drive straight over the *roundabout,* another *quarter* of a mile and you're there!	*in diesem Fall · Autobahn* *Kreisverkehr* *Viertel*
F: *Turn first right* and left at the roundabout ...	*die erste rechts*
C: Okay. We'll see you there at eleven thirty then. Goodbye *for now.*	*einstweilen*

Telefunctions revised

Telling them who you want to speak to

Is there somebody in authority I can talk to?	Kann ich jemanden sprechen, der zuständig ist?
I was expecting to be connected with ...	Ich dachte, man würde mich mit ... verbinden.

Putting them through

If you like I'll put you through to the personnel department.	Wenn Sie wünschen, verbinde ich Sie mit der Personalabteilung.
I'll connect you with ...	Ich verbinde Sie mit ...
There's a Mr A for Mr B on the phone.	Da ist ein Herr A für Herrn B am Apparat.
Shall I transfer the call to your desk?	Soll ich das Gespräch auf Ihren Apparat legen?

Screening

Dr. Brain is extremely busy at present.	Dr. Brain ist im Augenblick sehr beschäftigt.
I'm afraid Mr Halfar is not available.	Herr Halfar ist leider nicht zu sprechen.
Can I take a message?	Kann ich etwas ausrichten?
Could you give me a few details about it?	Können Sie mir ein paar Einzelheiten geben?

Through to the boss

Andrew Goodman (**A**) *has managed* to get the phone-number of Dr. B. Brain (**B**). He wants to *take the risk* and talk to the boss directly. *"It's all or nothing"*, he thinks.	*ist es gelungen* · *das Risiko eingehen* · *alles oder nichts*
A: Good morning, is that Dr. Brian Brain of Robotalot?	
B: Yes, this is Brain speaking. What can I do for you?	
A: Actually, I hope *I'm not being too pushy* but I got your number from your receptionist. It's about the *post in sales* you are offering.	*ich bin nicht zu aufdringlich* · *Stelle als Verkäufer*
B: What?! You got my number from Jane Simpson. I've given *instructions* not to be *disturbed* until I've heard who the *callers* are. How did you *manage* that?	*Anweisungen* · *gestört* · *Anrufer* · *anstellen*
A: Actually, it's not Mrs Simpson's *fault*. When you really want to get information on the phone there are ways to get it. It's only a *matter* of saying the right words. It's like selling really.	*Schuld* · *eine Frage*
B: Yes, that's true. I wish my receptionist was as *efficient* as you are. Perhaps you've already *scored a few points*. So you want to come for an interview, do you? Can you be here tomorrow, Wednesday at ten o'clock?	*tüchtig* · *ein paar Punkte sammeln*
A: Certainly, sir! Could you *give me some directions*. I'm *not familiar with* the area.	*den Weg erklären* · *sich nicht auskennen*
B: You're coming by train, *I suppose*? Just leave the station at the *front exit*, the main door. Walk across the *crossing*, turn first right, walk along that road, about 100 metres, until you reach Belfort Street. Left along Belfort Street. It's number 15–18. I'd better end this conversation now. It's already *six a.m.* and I've got a full *schedule*. Good luck!	*annehmen* · *Vorderausgang* · *Kreuzung* · *sechs Uhr morgens* · *Terminkalender*

Speech functions: Finding the way to Robotalot

Asking your way	
Could you give me some directions?	Könnten Sie mir erklären, wie ich zu Ihnen komme?
Can you describe the way to me?	Könnten Sie mir den Weg beschreiben?
Could you tell me how to get there?	Könnten Sie mir sagen, wie ich dort hinkomme?
I'm coming by car/train.	Ich komme mit dem Auto/Zug.

Describing the way	
Leave the station at the front exit.	Verlassen Sie den Bahnhof durch den vorderen Ausgang.
Walk across the crossing.	Überqueren Sie die Kreuzung.
Take the first on the left/right.	Biegen Sie in die erste Straße links/rechts.
Walk along that road until you reach Belfort Street.	Gehen Sie die Straße entlang, bis Sie zur Belfortstraße kommen.
You drive off the motorway at the Nottingham sign.	Sie verlassen die Autobahn bei Ausfahrt Nottingham.
Turn second right.	Biegen Sie in die zweite rechts.
Drive straight ahead at the roundabout.	Fahren Sie geradeaus über den Kreisverkehr.

Time for a smile

Bob: Hello,Tim, it's me, Bob. I wonder if you would like to come to my house-warming party[1] on Saturday?

Tim: Thank-you. That's very nice of you. How do I get to your place?

Bob: Walk along Nelson Road until you reach Wilton Crescent. I live opposite the post office, number 32, second floor. Just push[2] the bell[3] with your nose[4].

Tim: Why with my nose?

Bob: You're not coming empty-handed[5], are you?

1 Einweihungsparty 2 drücken 3 Klingel 4 Nase 5 mit leeren Händen

Your Teletrainer

EXERCISE 1: Describe the way from the station to the Ritz

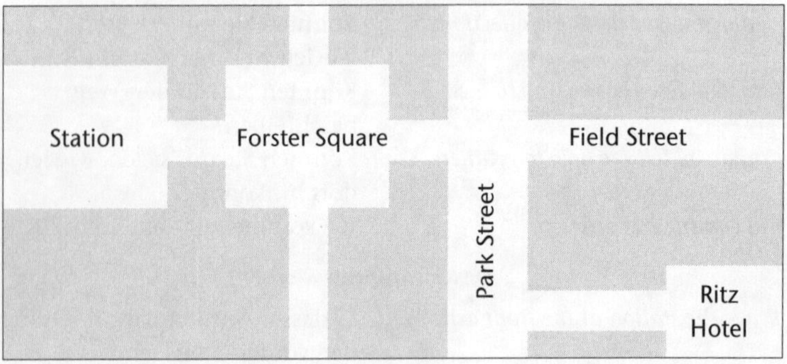

EXERCISE 2: Give each line its correct number

Child:	*I'm afraid Dr. Brain is not available at the moment. Can I take a message?*	*2*
Knox:	*My name is Knox, like Fort Knox in the States.*	
Knox:	*It's about that advertisement in the Late News.*	
Knox:	*Good afternoon. I'd like to speak to Dr. Brain, if that is possible.*	
Knox:	*Yes, that's it.*	
Child:	*I see. It's in connection with the post of a salesman we've advertised, isn't it?*	
Child:	*Hold the line please, I'm putting you through.*	
Child:	*In that case I'll transfer you to the personnel department. Who shall I say is calling?*	

EXERCISE 3: Correct Mimi's English

Tom: *Excuse me, do you speak English?*
Mimi: *Yes, I've it in the school gelearnt .*
Tom: *Hm ... Could you tell me how to get to the station, please?*
Mimi: *Naturally. Go you just out and cross you the park. Then see you already the station. It is the big house before you.*
Tom: *What? Hm ... thank you very much indeed. Goodbye.*

Teletactics: How to avoid rush hours and secretaries

You might have wondered why Andrew got through to the boss *immediately*, why Dr. Brain took Andrew's call and not his secretary, whose job it is	*sich fragen* *sofort*
• to screen the director from callers,	
• to control his *agenda*,	*Terminkalender*
• and to plan the *appointments*.	*Termine*
Well, Andrew Goodman followed another good *piece of advice* in that book about telephoning (you *remember* the title?):	*Ratschlag* *sich erinnern*
1. Andrew was clever enough to get important information from Jane Simpson (page 52): Dr. Brain arrives at the office before his secretary and *prefers* to work late in the evening when he is alone in the office.	*vorziehen*
2. Andrew tried several times in the morning before the secretary had arrived. And as an early riser Dr. Brain obviously *appreciates* people who have *similar working habits* to his own.	*schätzen* *ähnliche Arbeitsgewohnheiten*

Time for a smile

After having watched the show for one hour René called the television studio:
"Excuse me, sir, do you think that the pop group playing in your live show would fulfill a wish of one of your most loyal[1] viewers[2]?
"With pleasure[3], sir. What would you like ?"
"Well, tell them to play table tennis for a change[4]."

1 treu 2 Zuschauer 3 mit Vergnügen 4 zur Abwechslung

Teletactics: Market studies on the phone

Do you know what your clients think this year about your company and your products? If you don't know but wanted to, you could *commission* an expensive *market survey* to find out your position on the market; you could start a *direct-mail* campaign and hope that your letters will be answered. Of course that would cost you a *packet*. You could, however, do it the cheap way: via telephone. Train those persons of your *staff* (secretaries, salesmen, receptionists ...) who do a lot of telephoning and teach them:

1. to ask the right questions and to find out the callers' *attitude* towards your products;
2. to *encourage* your clients to be honest and to criticise where they think it *justified*. *Suggestions* how to improve your products and *services* should be taken down in writing;
3. how to *flatter* critical clients on their *expertise;*
4. to *take notes* and to *promise prompt action* in case of complaints;
5. to thank the callers for the time they took to answer questions.

in Auftrag geben
Marktstudie
Postwurfsendung
eine Stange
Personal
Einstellung
ermutigen
gerechtfertigt · Anregungen
Dienstleistungen
schmeicheln
Fachkenntnis
Notizen machen · Sofortmaßnahmen versprechen

Time for a smile

It was three o'clock in the morning when Fred's phone rang. It was his doctor who he had sold a robot to. " My Tin Lizzy seems to have broken down. Could you please come at once to fix[1] it?" Fred reluctantly[2] agreed, but added[3] "I'm sorry, but at this time of night you can only expect a doctor's treatment[4]."
When Fred arrived, he went to the kitchen, threw three tablets into one of the robot's slots[5] and said to the doctor. "If it's not better by lunchtime phone me and I'll come again."

1 reparieren 2 widerwillig 3 hinzufügen 4 Behandlung 5 Schlitz

A HAPPY MESSAGE

CONTENTS

Our Telestory:	**A happy message**
Telefunctions:	**Taking and leaving messages**
Teletiquette:	**Taking messages**
Speech functions:	**Congratulating people**
Your Teletrainer:	**Messages and congratulations**
Our Telejokes:	**Time for a smile**

Time for a smile

It was already late in the evening, Jacky Brain had been waiting for her husband for quite a while. Finally she picked up the receiver[1] and called his office. A sweet young voice[2] answered the phone:

Jacky: I want to speak Dr. Brain and don't tell me he isn't in.
Voice: I beg your pardon, I didn't catch your name.
Who shall I say is calling?
Jacky: I'm his wife.
Voice: Are you? I'm his secretary.
Jacky: Were you?

1 Hörer 2 Stimme

A happy message

The interview *took place* last Wednesday. Andrew didn't feel *confident* afterwards. His girlfriend Fussy is at Andrew's appartment when the news arrives.	*stattfinden* · *zuversichtlich*
Fussy (F), Dr. Halfar (H)	
F: Hi, this is Fussy, who's that?	
H: How do you do? My name's Halfar from Robotalot. I'd like to speak to Mr Goodman *if that's possible.*	*wenn es möglich ist*
F: Well, I'm terribly sorry but *unfortunately* he's out at the moment. Can I take a *message*?	*leider* · *Nachricht*
H: Yes, but are you a *relative* of Mr Goodman? I mean it's a private *matter.*	*Verwandte* · *Angelegenheit*
F: Oh, that's no problem. He's not allowed to have *secrets* from me. I'm his girlfriend, or *rather* he's my boyfriend.	*Geheimnisse* · *vielmehr*
H: Okay. Mr Goodman has been *blessed* with the *good fortune* of *being awarded the post* of salesman at ...	*gesegnet* · *Glück · den Posten bekommen*
F: Are you trying to tell me that he's got the job?	
H: Yes, he has. Would you be so kind as to pass the *happy message* on to him?	*frohe Botschaft*

Time for a smile

The landlord[1] of the pub was wakened by the phone at three o'clock in the morning. "What time do you open?" asked the caller. "Half past ten," snapped[2] the landlord, and slammed[3] the phone down. This went on four more times, till the landlord protested: "Look, I'm trying to get some sleep. Can't you wait to get in?"
"I'm not trying to get in," cried the caller. "I'm trying to get out!"

1 Besitzer, Wirt 2 schnauzen 3 den Hörer auf die Gabel knallen

Telefunctions: Taking and leaving messages

How to take messages	
Can I take a message?	Kann ich etwas ausrichten?
Could I pass a message on to Mr Brain?	Könnte ich Herrn Brain irgend etwas ausrichten?
Would you like to leave a message for him?	Möchten Sie ihm eine Nachricht hinterlassen?
I'll make sure that he gets your message.	Ich werde dafür sorgen, daß er Ihre Nachricht erhält.

Leaving a message	
Could I leave a message, please?	Könnte ich eine Nachricht hinterlassen?
Would you please tell him that Bob called?	Würden Sie ihm bitte ausrichten, daß Bob angerufen hat?
Would you give John a message for me?	Würden Sie John etwas von mir ausrichten?
Would you be so kind as to pass the message on to him?	Wären Sie so freundlich, meine Nachricht an ihn weiterzugeben?
Can I leave a note for him?	Kann ich ihm eine Nachricht hinterlassen?
Could you let him know that I won't be free today?	Würden Sie ihm bitte ausrichten, daß ich heute keine Zeit habe?

Time for a smile

Homophones[1] are words that sound alike, for example, herd (Herde) and heard (hörte). On the telephone they are often the cause[2] of sad misunderstandings[3], as the following story shows:
"Hi Tim. It's me, Sue. You must come quickly. A bunch[4] of cows has broken into our garden." Tim: "Not 'bunch' – herd[5]!" Sue: "Heard[6] what?" Tim: "Herd of cows!" – Sue: "No – a cow herd!" Tim: "Why should I care what a cow heard? I've no secrets[7] from a cow."

1 gleichlautende Wörter 2 Ursache 3 Mißverständnisse 4 Haufen, Strauß 5 Herde 6 hörte 7 Geheimnisse

Teletiquette: Taking messages

"One moment, please I'll get pencil and paper." Don't use this telefunction. It makes a very bad impression: you are *disorderly*, you *misplace* things, you aren't prepared for answering phone calls.	*unordentlich* · *verlegen*
So don't pick up the *receiver* before you've got pencil and *notepad*.	*Hörer* · *Notizblock*
• Make sure that you have all the important figures (*orders, deadlines*).	*Aufträge · Fristen*
• Repeat numbers.	
• *Summarize* and *confirm* dates and deadlines;	*zusammenfassen · bestätigen*
• Thus you *avoid misunderstandings* and later complaints.	*Mißverständnisse vermeiden*
• Ask the caller to confirm that he is satisfied with your *summary*.	*Zusammenfassung*

Speech functions: Congratulating people

Fussy wants to congratulate Andrew on his success at Robotalot. She can choose between the following speech functions:

I've got to congratulate you.	Ich muß dir gratulieren.
I want to offer you my best wishes.	Ich möchte dir meine Glückwünsche überbringen.
You couldn't have done better.	Du hättest es nicht besser machen können.
Congratulations!	Herzlichen Glückwunsch!
Full marks!	Ausgezeichnet!
Well done!	Gut gemacht!
It's great / terrific!	Es ist einfach toll!
I'd like to compliment you on your achievement.	Meine Anerkennung für deine Leistung.

Fussy phones Andrew's pub

Fussy (**F**), Andrew (**A**)

F: Hello, is that the Black Duck? I think you've got a customer there called Andrew Goodman. Could you *page* him for me?	*ausrufen*
A: *(One minute later.)* Hello, Andrew Goodman speaking, who's there?	
F: Andrew, it's me, Fussy. *Guess* what? I've got to congratulate you.	*raten*
A: What about? There's not much to congratulate me about at the moment. Nothing much seems to be going right.	
F: You're a fully qualified and fully employed salesman *as of today.*	*von heute an*
A: What are you talking about? I'm *unemployed* and frustrated.	*arbeitslos*
F: You're a bit slow today. I'm trying to *offer* you my best wishes in your new job.	*hier: zum Ausdruck bringen*
A: Do you mean Robotalot have *accepted* me?	*hier: einstellen*
F: Of course. Congratulations! Well done! And I'm sure you'll do well in future.	
A: Well, that's a *turn-up for the books.* Fussy, jump into a taxi and shoot over here and we'll *celebrate.*	*eine gute Nachricht, Überraschung*; *feiern*

Time for smile

A Hollywood Actress who had been married and divorced[1] seven times, sent her daughter the following telegram to congratulate her on the occasion[2] of her wedding[3]:

BEST WISHES FOR A HAPPY AND SUCCESSFUL[4] FIRST MARRIAGE

1 geschieden 2 anläßlich 3 Hochzeit 4 erfolgreich

Your Teletrainer

EXERCISE 1: Complete the congratulations

Three men were waiting in the hospital waiting-room when the nurse came from the maternity ward[1]. She said to the first man, "Congratulations, you're the father of twins[2]. W . . . . !" – "Wonderful", he exclaimed. "Isn't that a coincidence[3]? I'm member of the Minnesota Twins baseball team!"
After a while the nurse returned and said to the second man, "Congratulations, you're the father of triplets[4]. F . . . m . . . . !" "Wow," said the new father, "another coincidence, I work for the 3M Company." The third man went pale[5] and said to the nurse, " Excuse me, could you get me a tranquilizer[6]? I work for 7-Up."

EXERCISE 2: Leaving a message (fill in the blanks)

Andrew: This is Andrew Goodman speaking. Could you . . . . Mr Halfar, please?
Jane: I'm sorry, he . . . ' . . . the company today.
Andrew: Could you . . . . a . . . . for him?
Jane: Sure.
Andrew: Could you . . . . him that I'm very happy that I got the job. Please . . . him if he could arrange a meeting with somebody who would explain the robot to me.
Jane: OK. I'll . . . . your . . . . to him.
Andrew: Thanks a lot.
Jane: You're . . . .

EXERCISE 3: Taking a message

Bob: Hello?
Tom: I wonder if I can speak to Jane, please?
Bob: Sorry, she isn't here. I . . . . a . . . . if you like.
Tom: Could you just . . . her k . . . that I won't be free for dinner tonight. We've got an important visitor.
Bob: I' ll g . . . her the m . . . . . . as soon as she comes back.

---

1 Entbindungsstation 2 Zwillinge 3 Zufall 4 Drillinge 5 blaß 6 Beruhigungsmittel

A JOB INTERVIEW ON THE PHONE

CONTENTS

Our Telestory:	**Fred Niemec gets a job**
Telefunctions:	**Interrupting on the phone**
Your Teletrainer:	**Let's practise spelling**
Teletactics:	**Spot the tactical mistakes**
Teletiquette:	**Can you spell your name?**
Your Teledoc:	**Why we interrupt.**
Our Telejokes:	**Time for a smile**

Time for a smile

An Irish priest rang up the police: "Hello, this is Father Benedict speaking. We've got a problem. There's a dead donkey[1] lying in front of my church. Could you please remove[2] it?"
The officer who took the call thought he would be smart[3]: "I thought it was the Church that took care[4] of the dead," he said.
"You are right, son," replied Father Benedict, "but first we have got to get in touch[5] with their relatives[6]."

1 Esel 2 entfernen 3 clever, witzig 4 sich kümmern um 5 sich in Verbindung setzen mit 6 Verwandte

A job interview on the phone

Fred Niemec was not *successful* in his application for a job at Robotalot. So he *kept on trying* and *eventually* had some success with Tin-Lizzy Inc., a *competitor* that offers a rather low quality *multi-purpose robot.*	*erfolgreich* *weiter versuchen* *schließlich* *Konkurrent* *Mehrzweckroboter*
Receptionist (**R**), Fred Niemec (**F**), Blocker (personnel director) (**B**)	
R: Hello, Tin-Lizzy Inc. here. What can I do for you?	
F: Well, I was thinking of applying for a job ...	
R: Oh, right! We've been looking for somebody for *quite some time.* I think the boss will take anybody, so *you might be in luck.*	*geraume Zeit* *Sie könnten Glück haben*
F: Well, do you think you can put me through?	
R: Of course, sir. Hold the line *(one minute later.)*	
B: Blocker speaking, yes?	
F: My name's Niemec. I'm phoning about your job. I want to apply for ...	
B: Now just a moment ... You want to *apply* for my job!? You wouldn't want my job. The personnel director is the most *hated* person ...	*sich bewerben* *verhaßt*
F: Excuse me, but you misunderstood me. I want the job of salesman for your line of robots.	
B: I see. Now could you *spell* your name? I'm not sure if I've got it right.	*buchstabieren*
F: Yes, of course. N.I.E.M.E.C. I think it's of Polish origin.	
B: Well, It's certainly not English, that's for sure. Now, tell me about yourself, young man.	
F: Well, I worked as a teacher for several years.	
B: Don't worry about that! We won't *hold it against* you.	*negativ auslegen*
F: And then I realized I was *wasting my time* and decided to try the private sector.	*Zeit verschwenden*

B: A very wise *decision*, my boy. And you're a good *talker*. That's what a salesman must be. I'm afraid I'll have to *cut this short*. I'm *hard pressed for time*. Now could I ask you to call me back tomorrow?	*Entscheidung* *Redner* *Schluß machen* *unter Zeitdruck*
F: Oh! Well fine. But was that really all?	
B: *Short and sweet*, my boy. Keep things short and sweet! I'll have *to leave* you now. I've got a full schedule. Until tomorrow then. By the way, you can reach me at this number: 60 77 81 4. Goodbye.	*kurz und bündig* *sich verabschieden*

Telefunctions: Interrupting on the phone

Unterbrechen, um zu korrigieren	
Now just a moment!	Moment mal!
Could I just break in here?	Könnte ich dazu kurz etwas sagen?
Excuse me for interrupting you, but ...	Entschuldigen Sie, wenn ich unterbreche, aber ...
I' m afraid I must interrupt you.	Ich muß Sie leider unterbrechen.

Unterbrechen aus Zeitnot	
I'm afraid I'll have to cut this short.	Ich muß das Gespräch leider abbrechen.
I'm hard pressed for time.	Ich bin unter Zeitdruck.
I've got a full schedule.	Ich habe ein volles Programm.
I'll have to leave you now.	Ich muß nun Schluß machen.

Eine Alternative anbieten	
Can I call you back, when I've more time?	Kann ich Sie zurückrufen, wenn ich etwas mehr Zeit habe?
Could I ask you to call me back?	Könnten Sie mich bitte zurückrufen?
You can reach me at this number.	Sie erreichen mich unter dieser Nummer.
You can contact me by car phone.	Sie erreichen mich über mein Autotelefon.
I'll be available till 3 p.m.	Ich bin bis 15 Uhr zu erreichen.

Your Teletrainer

EXERCISE 1: Correct the words in italics

Mimi rang the hotel manager: "This is John Doorbar speaking. Good morning. What can I ..." "Sorry to *underbreak* you. Come quickly." Five minutes later: "It's *unpossible*!" she complained when the manager arrived. "In the room *againstover* there is a man doing gymnastics – *fully* naked."
The manager looked out of the window – then he said: "Well, it's true. There is a man, but I can only see his head. You must be ..."
"*Unsense*!" interrupted Mimi angrily. "You just stand on this chair!"

EXERCISE 2: Spelling exercise

On page 182 you will find the British telephone alphabet.
Use it to spell the following words:
a) Tin Lizzy b) Robotalot c) Brain

EXERCISE 3: Translation exercise

Read or listen to the dialogue again and you won't have problems translating this dialogue.

S: Sam Spade, **H**: Dr. Halfar

H: Firma Robotalot. Guten Tag. Was kann ich für Sie tun?
S: Ich rufe wegen Ihrer Annonce an. Ich möchte mich für Ihre Stelle bewerben und ...
H: Einen Augenblick ... für meine Stelle? Aber das ist doch ...
S: Entschuldigen Sie bitte, wenn ich Sie unterbreche. Sie haben mich mißverstanden. Natürlich für die Stelle als Verkäufer Ihrer Roboter.
H: Sie haben Glück. Wir suchen schon seit geraumer Zeit jemanden. Kann ich Sie zurückrufen, wenn ich etwas mehr Zeit habe? Wie war doch gleich Ihr Name?
S: Spade, Sam Spade
B: Lassen Sie mich buchstabieren, um sicherzugehen.

Teletactics: Spot the tactical mistakes

The persons in the above conversation have made at least three tactical *mistakes*.

1. The receptionist is *indiscreet*. ("We've been looking for somebody for quite some time. I think the boss will take anybody"). *Thus* Niemec *learns* that he is in a good position.
2. Blocker is not a good *listener*. He is hard pressed for time. However, by interrupting Niemec he is only wasting time. ("Now, just a moment..."). See also Your Teledoc (page 78)
3. You don't interview or *hire* people over the telephone. (Fred: "But was that really all?" – "Keep things short and sweet.")

Fehler
indiskret
auf diese Weise
erfährt
Zuhörer
einstellen

Teletiquette: Can you spell your name?

There is one word most people like to hear: their own name – but only if it's *pronounced* properly and in a friendly tone. Let's go back to our telephone conversation. What is wrong with Blocker's question "Now could you spell your name?" Of course you can spell your name. If there is one word that you can write, it's your name. So, don't make people spell their names. It isn't *polite*. Do it yourself. Here's an example:

"Excuse me, Mr Kleinschroth, I just want to make sure that I got your name right. Does it have a 'th' at the end?"

"Excuse me, Dr. Moos, may I just spell your name to check whether I got it right: M, double O, S."

If a name is very complicated, or if the line is bad you use the international alphabet to spell a word *(see page 182)*.

aussprechen
höflich

Don't make *remarks* on the origin or meaning of a name: ("It's certainly not English, that's for sure"). Avoid *comparing* names with animals or *tools* ("How do you spell you name Mr Spade, like the *spade* in my garden? Let's call a spade a spade ha ha ha").

Bemerkungen · *vergleichen* · *Geräte* · *Spaten*

Your Teledoc: Why do we interrupt?

We learn to speak, read and write. But we don't learn to listen. However, listening *skills* are essential to international business. On the telephone, this skill is *particularly* important, because we don't get the physical information, the *body language*, for example. In the following chapters your teledoc will present the most important listening techniques.

Fertigkeiten · *besonders* · *Körpersprache*

Why do people interrupt? The *average* person speaks about 150 words per minute, while the listener's brain can *absorb* about 400 words per minute. What do we do with this extra capacity? Nothing. That's why the *unskilled* listener becomes *bored* and *tends* to interrupt.

Durchschnitts- · *aufnehmen* · *ungeübt* · *gelangweilt · neigen*

The skilled listener is never bored. He uses this extra capacity to listen and to analyse the meaning of the words. He wants to understand fully. Instead of interrupting he *encourages* the speaker to go on in his talk. How to encourage a caller, how to analyse his words is *subject* of another chapter. So long!

ermutigen · *Thema, Gegenstand*

APPOINTMENT WITH A POTENTIAL CUSTOMER

CONTENTS

Our Telestory:	**Appointment with a potential customer**
Speech functions:	**Getting together**
Your Teletrainer:	**Mixed exercises**
Your Teledoc:	**Getting to know the "visual caller"**
Our Telejokes:	**Time for a smile**

Time for a smile

Andrew Goodman was a bit annoyed[1] when his neighbour[2] phoned him at 4 a.m. and said, "Your dog is barking[3] so loudly that I can't sleep." Before Andrew could say anything the neighbour had hung up[4].
The following morning, at the same time, Andrew phoned his neighbour and said, "By the way[5], I haven't got a dog."

1 verärgert 2 Nachbar 3 bellen 4 auflegen, einhängen 5 übrigens

Appointment with a potential customer

So now we have Andrew Goodman and Fred Niemec, two young salesmen *in competition with* each other. Andrew seems to be with a good company and a good product, Fred with Tin Lizzy and a "cowboy" *outfit*. Tin Lizzy is also the name of their robot. Now the real work must begin. The two salesmen try to sell their wares. Andrew Goodman has heard about a *potential customer* in Scotland. He has to make an *initial phone-call*.

im Wettbewerb
Crew, Bande
potentieller Kunde
ein erstes Telefongespräch

Secretary (**S**), Andrew (**A**), Mr Brodie (**B**)

S: Hello, Domestic Services. Miss McGregor speaking. *Can I be of assistance*?

Kann ich Ihnen helfen

A: Well, I very much hope so. You see your company has been *recommended* to me as a very *reliable* one.

empfehlen
zuverlässig

S: We'd certainly like to think so, sir. *How can I help you further*?

Was kann ich noch für Sie tun?

A: Well, thank you very much. *It's in connection with* a new product for you. It's very important that I *get into contact with* the director of the *purchasing department*. You see we've had the *good fortune* to have developed an all-round robot specially for *domestic services*.

Es handelt sich um
sich in Verbindung setzen mit · *Einkauf*
Glück
Haushaltsarbeit

S: I understand, sir. Of course, you'll need to speak to Mr Brodie. He's the boss of our purchasing.

A: Could you possibly put me through to him?

S: Well, normally I shouldn't, but since it's so important I'll connect you.

B: Hello, can I help you?

A: Yes, I've been trying to get into contact with you for some time. We've been *watching* your *product line* and services and we're sure that we can *complement* your *offer*.

beobachten
Warenangebot
ergänzen · *Angebot*

B: I'm sorry, Mr.... eh, I didn't *catch* your name. Could you repeat it?	*verstehen*
A: Of course, I'm sorry. The *line is bad.* My name's Goodman. Andrew Goodman.	*Leitung ist schlecht*
B: Well, Mr Woodman I'd....	
A: Sorry to *break in.* It's Goodman. G-O-O-D and man. If I could just get back to our *solution,* it's a *multi-purpose, domestic* service robot. It does everything.	*unterbrechen* · *Lösung* · *Vielzweckhaushalts-*
B: I beg your pardon. We've got terrible *interference.* I'm not sure whether I got that right. Did you say 'multi-purpose domestic service'?	*Nebengeräusche*
A: No, no. It's a domestic robot. It does things *round the house.* We believe it's a perfect *complement to your range.*	*rund um das Haus · Ergänzung Ihrer Warenpalette*
B: Hmm. Okay. Perhaps we should have a short *meeting* together. When would it be *suitable* for you?	*Besprechung · passend*
A: Next Wednesday would suit me.	
B: Wednesday the 14th, you say. Let's make it the Wednesday, then. And what time shall we say? Would *5 p.m.* be alright?	*5 Uhr nachmittags*
A: Make it a bit later. *Let's say seven.* Maybe we could have a *working dinner.*	*sagen wir sieben* · *Arbeitsessen*
B: Good idea. *I'd better let you* get on with your work. Goodbye.	*ich lasse Sie lieber ...*

Time for a smile

McNab, a real Scotsman, decided[1] to get married[2]. So one morning he sent telegrams to three of his girlfriends proposing marriage[3]. Two phoned to say "yes" immediately[4], and the third phoned that night to say the same. He married the third girl saying, "The girl for me is the one who waits for night rates[5]."

1 beschließen 2 heiraten 3 Heiratsantrag machen 4 sofort 5 Nachttarif

Speech functions: Getting together

When can we get together?	Wann können wir uns treffen?
When would it suit you?	Wann paßt es Ihnen?
We could meet up tomorrow.	Wir könnten uns morgen treffen.
Let's make it Wednesday then.	Sagen wir also Mittwoch.
And at what time?	Und um welche Uhrzeit?
When would be a good time?	Wann wäre es für Sie günstig?
Would five p.m. be alright?	Würde Ihnen 17 Uhr passen?
What about 7 p.m.?	Wie wär's mit 19 Uhr?
Make it a bit later.	Sagen wir etwas später.
Let's say seven a.m.	Sagen wir 7 Uhr (vormittags).
We could have a working lunch.	Wir könnten uns zu einem Arbeitsessen treffen.
I'm afraid I must cancel our appointment.	Ich muß unseren Termin leider absagen.

Your Teletrainer

EXERCISE 1: Wie haben es die Gesprächspartner gesagt?

What did they say for ... ?	*They said : ....*
Can I help you?	*Can I ....?*
What else can I do for you?	*How ....?*
It's about a new product.	*It's ....*
Could you possibly put me in contact with him?	*Could you possibly ....?*
Sorry to interrupt you.	*...........................*
The connection is bad.	*The .... is bad.*

EXERCISE 2: Complete the joke

A patient phones up his doctor for an ....:

Nurse: *The doctor will be able to see you on May 7th.*
Patient: *Not sooner than that? I could be dead by then.*
Nurse: *Never mind, you can always ...... your appointment.*

EXERCISE 3: What to say when the line is bad (2)

Choose the most idiomatic response.
You don't understand the caller's name:

1. Sorry, I didn't — *a* *hear* / *b* *understand* / *c* *catch* — *your name.*

2. I'm not sure if I — *a* *got that right.* / *b* *got that correctly.* / *c* *heard that right.*

3. We've got terrible — *a* *contact* / *b* *interference.* / *c* *noise on the line.*

4. What did you say — *a* *your name was?* / *b* *was your name?* / *c* *your name?*

EXERCISE 4: Sie wollen sich telefonisch verabreden

Fragen Sie Herrn Brodie:	
wann es ihm paßt:	*When .... s... you?*
nach einer günstigen Uhrzeit:	*When would .. .. time?*
ob ihm 17 Uhr passen würde:	*Would 5 p.m .. a.....?*

Schlagen Sie vor:	
den nächsten Mittwoch	*Let's m... .. Wednesday.*
18 Uhr	*W... a.... 6 p.m.?*
ein Arbeitsessen	*We c.... h... a w...... d.....*

Bestätigen Sie:	
Mittwoch, den 1.05.	*W........ the ..... of May,*
um 18 Uhr im Codogan Hotel.	*at 6 .. .. the Codogan.*

Your Teledoc: Getting to know the visual caller

More and more business is done over the phone. If you want to be *successful* in telephone marketing you must speak your partner's *language*, be on his or her *wavelength*. But first you have to find out what type your business partner is. Is he or she a *visual*, an *auditive* or a *kinesthetic type*? How do you find out? Simply by "*watching*" their language. What else could you do on the phone? So, analyse the *vocabulary* they use?

erfolgreich · *Sprache* · *Wellenlänge* · *Augen-, Ohren-* · *Gefühlstyp* · *beobachten* · *Wortschatz*

Mrs Henry is the visual type. She *uses* a lot of expressions like: Can you show me ...? can you give me an idea...? that is a bit vague; bring some *light* ...; look at it from another *angle* etc. With Mrs Henry you should use *imagery* whenever it is possible. Tell her about *size, shape* and colours of your product. Use *concrete* not abstract words (I'll *describe* it, imagine, can you see it? get an *impression* ...) and you will both be on the same wavelength because you have a language *in common* – the only thing you can *share* with a person you know nothing about. Your language becomes a *mirror*. If Mrs Henry can *recognize* herself, she will *trust* you.

verwenden · *Licht* · *Blickwinkel* · *Bildersprache* · *Größe, Form* · *konkret* · *beschreiben* · *Eindruck* · *gemeinsam* · *teilen* · *Spiegel* · *erkennen* · *trauen*

The visual type is a *fast* speaker because he has to keep up with the pictures that come to his *mind*. Since a picture says more than a thousand words he needs a lot of words to *convey* it – don't interrupt. And give him time to see the imagery of your language in his *mind's eye*.

schnell · *Sinn, Geist* · *mitteilen* · *geistiges Auge*

In the following chapters you will read about the auditive and the kinesthetic type.

A TICKET TO SCOTLAND

CONTENTS

Our Telestory :	Getting a ticket to Glasgow
Telefunctions:	Sorry, wrong number
Speech functions:	Booking things
Your Teletrainer:	Let's practise functions
Your Teledoc:	Getting to know the auditive caller
Our Telejokes:	Time for a smile

Time for a smile

A woman phones a police-station.

Woman: Oh please, officer, you must help me. I've lost my husband[1].

Officer: Can you give us a description[2] of your husband, madam?

Woman: Well, he's one metre fourty tall, he weighs 85 kilos, he has got a big belly,[3] no hair, false teeth[4] ... oh forget[5] it, officer!

1 Ehemann 2 Beschreibung 3 Bauch 4 falsche Zähne 5 vergessen Sie es

Getting a ticket to Glasgow, Scotland

Robotalot is *located* just outside London. Andrew's potential customer is in Scotland. He must manage the *arrangements*.	*gelegen* / *Vorbereitungen*
Andrew (**A**), Information Clerk (**I**), Mr Smith (**S**), Operator (**O**)	
A: Hello, could I speak to the *information clerk*, please?	*Auskunft*
S: I'm sorry. You've got the wrong number. This is Mr Smith at the *town hall*. You must have *dialled the wrong number*.	*Rathaus* / *sich verwählen*
A: I don't understand ...	
S: What number are you trying to call?	
A: *British Rail*. 01 926 47111.	*Britische Bahn*
S: Well, we're 926 47711.	
A: Oh, I'm sorry, I'll try again.	
A: Hello, *operator*, could you give me the number of British Rail, please?	*Vermittlung*
O: Which city, please?	
A: Well, in London.	
O: P*assenger information* is 01 926 47111.	*Zugauskunft*
A: Well, I've just tried that number. Okay, thanks very much. (2 minutes later)	
I: Hello, British Rail speaking. How can I help you?	
A: Yes, I'd like some information about *train departures*. Could you give me a few *times*? I'd like to arrive at about 8 a.m. on the 14th of September in Glasgow.	*Abfahrtszeiten der Züge*
I: Yes, sir, actually *you're in luck*. There's only one train and that arrives at 7.30 a.m. It *departs* from London Victoria at 22.10.	*Glück haben* / *abfahren*
A: Can I reserve a *sleeping compartment*?	*Schlafwagen*
I: Of course, sir, but you'd better *book* today.	*buchen*

Otherwise I can't guarantee you'll get a place. You'll have to come to the *station* to book the ticket.	*sonst* *Bahnhof*
A: Can't I do it over the phone?	
I: Sorry, sir. It's not possible. Too many *jokers* phoning through!	*Spaßvögel*

Telefunctions: Sorry, wrong number

You must have dialled the wrong number.	Sie müssen sich verwählt haben.
Sorry, this is the wrong extension.	Tut mir leid, dies ist nicht der richtige Apparat.
I'm sorry, but this is not the right department.	Tut mir leid, aber dies ist nicht die richtige Abteilung.
The number has been changed.	Die Rufnummer hat sich geändert.
This isn't the department you want.	Dies ist nicht die Abteilung, die Sie wünschen.
Who did you say you wanted to speak to?	Wen, sagten Sie, wollten Sie sprechen?
What number are you calling?	Welche Nummer haben Sie gewählt?
I was connected with / to the wrong department.	Ich bin mit der falschen Abteilung verbunden worden.
Sorry to have troubled you.	Entschuldigen Sie bitte die Störung.
Could you pass me back to the operator?	Könnten Sie mich wieder mit der Vermittlung verbinden?

Time for a smile

"Who was that on the phone?" asked the suspicious[1] wife. "It was a wrong number again, dear – this woman trying to call the MET Office[2], ... she wanted to know if the coast was clear[3]."

1 argwöhnisch 2 Wetteramt 3 ob an der Küste klare Sicht sei/ob die Luft rein sei

Speech functions: Booking things

I wonder if you could give me some information?	Könnten Sie mir wohl eine Auskunft geben?
Could you tell me the time of the first train to Glasgow?	Könnten Sie mir sagen, wann der erste Zug nach Glasgow geht?
I'd like to travel on the 21st.	Ich würde gerne am 21. fahren.
I'm afraid the flight is fully booked.	Ich fürchte, der Flug ist ausgebucht.
I'd like to book a table for tonight.	Ich würde gerne einen Tisch für heute Abend reservieren.
I'd like to reserve a ticket for Liverpool.	Ich möchte eine Fahrkarte nach Liverpool reservieren.
One moment, please. I'll see what there is.	Moment, bitte. Ich sehe nach, was noch frei ist.
And what's the price of a double room?	Und wie teuer ist ein Doppelzimmer?
Can I pay by credit card?	Kann ich mit Kreditkarte zahlen?

Your Teletrainer

EXERCISE 1: What do they answer?

This is the wrong

n . . . . .

d . . . . t

e . . . . n

EXERCISE 2: What do they ask?

W . . . number are you..................................?

W . . did you say you w............ to .... to?

EXERCISE 3: Translation exercise

Bob: Könnte ich bitte die Auskunft haben?
Rec: Tut mir leid. Falsch verbunden. Hier ist Firma Blight.
Bob: Das verstehe ich nicht.
Rec: Welche Nummer haben Sie denn gewählt?
Bob: British Rail. 01 926 47111. Entschuldigen Sie die Störung.

(*Bob tries again*)

Info: Zugauskunft. Guten Tag.
Bob: Guten Tag. Ich bräuchte ein paar Abfahrtszeiten. Ich möchte in Glasgow ungefähr um 6 Uhr ankommen.
Info: Es gibt nur einen Zug, und der kommt um 7.30 a.m. an. Er fährt von Victoria Station um 11.45 p.m. ab.
Bob: Vielen Dank. Auf Wiedersehen.

EXERCISE 4: Correct Mimi's English

Clerk: Hello, British Air speaking. Can I help you?
Mimi: Can you me informations give like I come after Canterbury?
Clerk: To Canterbury? I'm afraid you dialled the wrong number, Madam. This is British Air and not British Rail.
Mimi: What you not say! Air – Rail. This is the third meal that I a false number become. When endly become I the right number? Heretolands is everything so complicated.
Clerk: For British Rail dial 01 926 47111. Good luck!

Time for a smile

René phoned the information desk at Heathrow Airport:
"Could you please tell me how long the Concorde takes to get to Paris?"
"Just one moment, sir ..."
"Wow! Thank you very much" said René and hung up.

Your Teledoc: Getting to know the auditive caller

In the last chapter we had a look at Mrs Henry, the visual type. Mr Johnson, however, is the auditive type. He *enjoys listening* to himself rather than to what you have to say. So don't *interrupt* him:

gerne zuhören
unterbrechen

- Mr Johnson likes music; his melodious *voice* comes deep from his *chest*. Try to *imitate* him, but keep natural.

  Stimme
  Brust · nachahmen

- He is not a fast speaker like the visual type. His language has no pictures to transport, so he doesn't need a lot of words to *get his message across*.

  um zu sagen, was er sagen will

- He uses words that *describe* sounds and noises like: that *sounds* interesting; I understand clearly what you mean; I want to say; you *mentioned* ...; an inner voice tells me that ...; there are *rumours* that ...; they *announced* that ...; we don' t speak the same language ...; may I *summarise* ..., I was *speechless*; it's all very well for you to talk like that ...; I'm *all ears*; *mutual* understanding

  beschreiben
  klingen
  erwähnen
  Gerüchte
  ankündigen
  zusammenfassen
  sprachlos
  ganz Ohr · gegenseitig

If you want to make Mr Johnson feel at home and to come to a mutual understanding with him, don't use pictures, use *auditive* language: sounds, *noises*. And when you meet him, don't talk about your holiday in terms of the colours of the ocean when the sun was *setting*. Talk about the sounds the wind made in the trees and the *waves* on the *beach* and you will be on his wavelength.

akustisch
Geräusche
untergehen
Wellen · Strand

CAN I TAKE A MESSAGE?

CONTENTS

Our Telestory:	**He's out on business**
Telefunctions:	**Leaving and taking messages**
Your Teletrainer:	**Let's practise taking messages**
Teletactics:	**Let's analyse the diaologue**
Our Telejokes:	**Time for a smile**

Time for a smile

A Glasgow doctor to McNab on the phone: "Mr McNab! Last week I treated[1] you for arthritis[2], you paid by cheque! This morning the cheque came back."
"Well", said McNab, "This morning my athritis came back as well."

1 behandeln

He's out on business

Meanwhile Fred Niemec has also managed to find a *potential customer*. This customer is only 50 miles from London, where Tin Lizzy Inc. has its *headquarters*. He has to make his first telephone call to Hospital Services, in Middlesex.	*inzwischen* · *potentieller Kunde* · *Hauptniederlassung*
Receptionist (**R**), Fred Niemec (**F**)	
R: Hospital Services, reception, Good afternoon.	
F: Right. My name's Fred Niemec. I wonder if you could help me? Who's *in charge of* purchasing at your place?	*leiten*
R: Sorry, what do you mean *purchasing*?	*Einkauf*
F: I mean who buys *equipment* for your company to resell?	*Ausrüstung*
R: Oh, you want the Director of the *Buying Department*. Why didn't you say so? Can I take a message for him?	*Einkaufsabteilung*
F: I'm afraid not. It's a highly technical *matter*. I'm afraid it would take too long to explain that to you.	*Angelegenheit*
R: Maybe. Anyhow, he's away *on business*.	*geschäftlich*
F: Well, in that case could you pass on a *message* for me? You see *it's in connection with* a cheap multipurpose *laser-guided* hospital robot. You know what I mean? It does all ...	*Nachricht* · *sich handeln um* · *lasergesteuert*
R: Sorry to interrupt you, sir, I'm not sure if I got that right. I'll *repeat* that ... A robot for laser-guided hosp –	*wiederholen*
F: No, no, no ... a cheap laser-guided robot for multipurpose hospitals. Do you understand?	
R: I'm not sure I do. I'd better *take* that *down*. Just a moment, I'll get a pencil and paper.	*aufschreiben*

(after a some minutes)	
R: I would like to make sure that I understood that correctly. May I just *read back* the details: A cheap hospital guide for multipurpose ... laser robots ... Wait a minute ... or was it a robot hosp... ?	*vorlesen*
F: Oh forget it ... Could you just *let* him *know* that Fred Niemec, the computer consultant, called in connection with a multilaser ... ehm ... with a robot! Could you ask him to *phone me back* on 23 44 52?	*mitteilen* *zurückrufen unter Nummer*
R: I'll *pass* your message *on* to Mr Shark. I'll see that he gets it *as soon as* he comes back.	*weiterleiten* *sobald*
F: Thanks. Sorry, I've got to *rush*. I'm late for an appointment. Goodbye.	*sich beeilen*

Telefunctions: Leaving and taking messages (See also Chapter 8)

Saying that someone is out	**Sagen, daß jemand nicht da ist**
Mr Shark is out of the office at the moment.	Herr Shark ist im Augenblick nicht im Büro.
He isn't in yet.	Er ist noch nicht da.
I'm afraid Mr Brain is not available at the moment.	Herr Brain ist im Augenblick leider nicht erreichbar.
Mr Brain is away on business.	Herr Brain ist geschäftlich unterwegs.
He's in the middle of an interview for a job.	Er ist mitten in einem Vorstellungsgespräch.
He is at a meeting.	Er ist in einer Besprechung.
Mr Shark might be on his lunch break.	Herr Shark ist möglicherweise in der Mittagspause.
Could his secretary help you?	Kann seine Sekretärin Ihnen weiterhelfen?
Would you like to speak to someone else?	Möchten Sie mit jemand anderem sprechen?

Leaving a message	**Eine Nachricht hinterlassen**
Would it be possible to leave a message?	Wäre es möglich, eine Nachricht zu hinterlassen?
Could you give him a message?	Könnten Sie ihm etwas ausrichten?
Could you let him know that I'll call back tomorrow?	Könnten Sie ihm mitteilen, daß ich morgen zurückrufe?
Would you pass that on to Mr Shark?	Würden Sie das bitte an Herrn Shark weiterleiten?

Taking messages	**Nachrichten entgegennehmen**
I'd better take that down.	Ich notiere das lieber.
I'm not sure whether I got that right. I'll repeat that.	Ich bin nicht sicher, ob ich das richtig verstanden habe. Ich wiederhole.
I would like to make sure that I've understood that correctly.	Ich würde gerne sichergehen, daß ich alles richtig verstanden habe.
May I just read back the details?	Ich lese die Einzelheiten noch einmal vor.
I'll pass your message on to Mr Shark.	Ich gebe Ihre Nachricht an Herrn Shark weiter.
I'll see that he gets your message.	Ich sorge dafür, daß er Ihre Nachricht erhält.

Time for a smile

Misunderstandings on the phone are often caused by homophones (words with the same pronunciation) for example "not" and "knot":

Customer: I've a complaint to make. The boards[1] you delivered[2] last week are full of holes[3].

Salesman: They're knot holes[4], if you ask me. That's normal.

Customer: Are you kidding[5]? Well, if they're not holes, what are they?

1 Bretter 2 liefern 3 Löcher 4 Astlöcher 5 machen Sie Witze?

Your Teletrainer

EXERCISE 1: Find the telefunction in our dialogue that has the same meaning:

Could I leave a message?	*Would it .... leave a message?*
Could you tell him that I'll call back tomorrow?	*Could you .... that I'll call back tomorrow?*
Would you give Mr Shark a message for me?	*Would you ..... message .. to Mr Shark?*

EXERCISE 2: What to say when Mr Shark isn't in?

...... business

not ....

Mr Shark is

..... the office

... meeting

EXERCISE 3: Correct Mimi's English

Fred: *Tin Lizzy Limited, the company that offers the world's best robots. Good morning. What can I do for you?*

Mimi: *Yes. I have heard that you newerthings a house roboter to onbid have.*

Fred: *You mean our houshould robot. Let me explain to ...*

Mimi: *Excuse you me that I you underbreak. This is a farcall. I shout from Germany on. Only one question, can the robot cook?*

Fred: *Sure, it has been programmed by the French cook Baucuse.*

Mimi: *Very good. Can he also icebone with sauerkraut make?*

Fred: *Make what? You mean icecream with ... hm ... Well, sauerkraut shouldn't be a problem.*

EXERCISE 4: Guided Translation Exercise

Jane Simpson, Reception (J), Andrew Goodman (A)	
J: Tut mir leid, Andrew, Herr Dr. Halfar ist noch *im Urlaub*. Kann ich etwas ausrichten?	*on holiday*
A: Würden Sie Ihm bitte sagen, daß ich am dritten nach Glasgow zu Domestic Services fahre und ...	
J: Moment, bitte. Ich schreibe das lieber auf.	*had better note down*
A: ... und also erst in drei Tagen zurückkomme. Fragen Sie ihn, ob er die neuen *Prospekte* schon hat und ob er sie an Domestic Services *schicken* kann. Die Adresse liegt auf meinem *Schreibtisch*. *Haben* Sie das?	*brochure* *send* *desk* *get*
J: Ich wiederhole *sicherheitshalber* alles noch einmal.	*make sure*

Teletactics: Let's analyse Fred's phone-call

1. "It's in connection with a cheap multipurpose laser-guided hospital robot." Don't tell anybody that your products are cheap – they are good value for money.
2. "It's a highly technical matter. I'm afraid it would take too long to explain that to you." This is offensive. Well-trained receptionists understand a lot about their company's products.
3. "Sorry, I've got to rush. I'm late for an appointment." Don't give the impression that you are hard-pressed for time. On the telephone it's worse than in a face to face situation. And don't admit that you are late for appointments. Some managers rely on their receptionists' or secretaries' first impressions.
4. "Who's in charge of purchasing at your place?" Don't call their company a "place".
5. "Could you ask him to phone me back?" Don't ask a potential customer to return your call. Ask when it would be convenient for the customer to be called back by you.

SHARK IS KEEN ON[1] LIZZY

CONTENTS

Our telestory:	**Fixing up a meeting with Fred and Lizzy**
Telefunctions:	**Starting and ending calls**
Your Teletrainer:	**Let's practise telefunctions**
Teletactics:	**Terminating calls effectively**
Our Telejokes:	**Time for a smile**

Time for a smile

A long distance phone-call

A young lady was permitted[2] by her parents to take employment[3] in London and live in her own apartment. The one condition[4] was that she would not allow gentleman friends in her apartment. "It would worry[5] me a lot!", said her mother.
During a long distance phone-call[6], the daughter described her date[7] of the previous evening[8] to her mother.
"You didn't permit[9] that man in your flat, did you?" asked the nervous mother. – "Oh, no!" replied the daughter, "we went to his flat. Let his mother worry[10]."

1 scharf sein auf 2 ihr wurde erlaubt 3 eine Stelle annehmen 4 Bedingung 5 sich sorgen 6 Ferngespräch 7 Rendezvous 8 Vorabend 9 erlauben 10 Soll sich doch seine Mutter Sorgen machen

Fixing up a meeting with Fred and Lizzy

Two days later Fred Niemec *receives* a phone-call from Hospital Services. It's the *Purchasing Manager*, Mr Shark.

erhalten · *Einkaufsleiter*

Purchasing Manager (**P**), Fred (**F**)

P: Shark here from Hospital Services. I got your message and I'm phoning back. I'm happy to have found you. You didn't *leave* your name. You're Mr ...

hinterlassen

F: Yes, my name's Niemec. I'm really glad to get hold of you. I *represent* Tin Lizzy Inc., one of the *major manufacturers* of domestic service robots, our Tin Lizzy *range*.

vertreten · *größerer Hersteller* · *Produktpalette*

P: And you think we'd be interested in your Lizzy. So what's so special about it?

F: I *suppose* the *main thing* is that it has so many functions. You can use it *anywhere* in the hospital. It keeps everybody happy.

annehmen · *Hauptsache* · *überall*

P: That sounds *promising*. But what exactly does it do?

vielversprechend

F: It cleans floors, *gives injections*, makes beds, takes the *lunches*. Anything you want. And it's *cheap*. Although it's hi-tech, it's still very cheap. I'd like to make an appointment with you to demonstrate its *qualities*.

Spritzen geben · *Mittagessen* · *billig* · *Eigenschaften*

P: Okay. So let's *fix up a meeting*. Would next Wednesday, 24th August, be okay?

Termin vereinbaren

F: Absolutely. I'll certainly be there.

P: Well, then I'll let you get on with your work. *I'm looking forward to* meeting your Tin Lizzy. I must *confess* that robots are my hobby.

ich freue mich auf · *gestehen*

F: Thank-you for calling. It was nice to hear from you.

Telefunctions: Starting and ending calls

Starting conversations	**Gespräche einleiten**
I'm really glad to get hold of you.	Ich freue mich sehr, daß ich Sie erreiche.
Ah, Mr Brain. This is an unexpected pleasure.	Ah, Herr Brain, das ist aber eine freudige Überraschung.
I'm glad that I've found you.	Ich bin froh, daß ich Sie ausfindig machen konnte.
I'm pleased I managed to get in touch with you.	Ich bin froh, daß es mir gelungen ist, Sie zu erreichen.
I wonder if you can spare me a minute.	Hätten Sie wohl eine Minute Zeit?
I hope I'm not disturbing you.	Ich hoffe, ich störe nicht.
This is Tom Smith returning your call.	Tom Smith am Apparat. Ich sollte Sie zurückrufen.
You left a message asking me to call you back.	Sie ließen mir ausrichten, ich möchte Sie zurückrufen.
I'm glad you called back so soon.	Ich freue mich, daß Sie so schnell zurückgerufen haben.
Thanks for calling me back.	Vielen Dank für Ihren Rückruf.
Thank-you for returning my call.	Danke, daß Sie zurückgerufen haben.

Ending conversations	**Gespräche beenden**
Thank-you for calling.	Vielen Dank für Ihren Anruf.
I'd better let you get on with your work.	Ich lasse Sie nun lieber weiterarbeiten.
It was nice to hear from you.	Hat mich gefreut, von Ihnen zu hören.
It's been a pleasure talking to you.	Es war mir eine Freude, mich mit Ihnen zu unterhalten.
Could I phone you when I've more time?	Kann ich Sie anrufen, wenn ich etwas mehr Zeit habe?
I'm afraid I'll have to cut this short. I'm hard-pressed for time.	Ich fürchte, ich muß es kurz machen. Ich stehe unter Zeitdruck.

Your Teletrainer

EXERCISE 1: Which functions are used in (almost) the same situation?

For example, 2 and f go together

1 I'm glad you called back so soon.	*a It was nice to hear from you.*
2 I hope I'm not disturbing you but ...	*b Can I get back to you when I'm not so busy?*
3 This is Tom Smith returning your call.	*c I'm pleased I managed to get in touch with you.*
4 I'm really glad to get hold of you.	*d You left a message asking me to call you back.*
5 It's been a pleasure talking to you.	*e Thank-you for returning my call so soon.*
6 Could I phone you when I've more time?	*f I'm sorry to phone you like this, but ...*

EXERCISE 2: Reasons for ending a call

I'm hard p . . . . . d for time

I've got a v . . . . . r

I've got a full s . . . . e

I must cut this short.

I'm in the middle of an i . . . . w.

I've got to a . . . . d a m . . . . . g

I've got a train to c . . . .

EXERCISE 3: Correct Mimi's English

Mimi had won a cruise[1] on big a luxury liner[2]. She was especially fond[3] of the excellent food. One night she managed to be put through to the head chef[4] in the kitchen:
"Have you a moment time for me. I must you say how wonderful your Beef Bourguignon was. Can you give me the äh Rezept, ... the recipe?"
"Certainly, madam," said the chef. "First you take twelve hundred onions[5], fourty bottles of wine ... are you still with me, madam?"

EXERCISE 4: Translation

A conversation between Goodman (**G**) and Brodie (**B**).

B: *Ah, Herr Goodman, das ist aber eine freudige Überraschung.*
G: *Guten Tag, Herr Brodie. Ich freue mich sehr, daß ich Sie erreicht habe. Hätten Sie wohl eine Minute Zeit?*
B: *Aber sicher. Was kann ich für Sie tun?*
G: *Ich hoffe, ich störe nicht, aber es ist dringend (urgent). Könnten wir unser Treffen auf den Donnerstag verschieben (put off)?*
B: *Das paßt mir gut. Aber ich muß leider Schluß machen. Ich muß zu unserer wöchentlichen Produktionsbesprechung. Bis Donnerstag also.*

Time for a smile

There was no doubt[6] about it. Anne was pregnant[7].
"Please feel free to use my telephone if you'd like to ring up your husband," said the doctor.
"But doctor, I'm not married."
"Well then, you'd better phone up your lover[8]."
"But, doctor, I've never had a lover!"
"All right. Then I must ask you to call your mother and tell her to get ready[9] for the second coming[10] of Jesus Christ."

1 Kreuzfahrt 2 Kreuzfahrtschiff 3 sehr mögen 4 Küchenchef 5 Zwiebel 6 Zweifel
7 schwanger 8 Liebhaber 9 sich vorbereiten auf 10 Wiederkehr

Teletactics: Terminating calls effectively

How to get *notorious chatterboxes* off the line. To some telephone *addicts*, the polite telefunctions "Could I phone you up when I've more time?" are only invitations to *engage* you in another thirty minutes of small talk. In this case we *advise* the following tactics:	*gefürchtete Schwatzbasen* · *(Drogen-)Abhängiger* · *verwickeln* · *raten*
1. *Invent emergencies*	*erfinden · Notfall*
First example: "I've just had a note put in front of me saying that the managing director has *called* a meeting which starts in two minutes and *I'm expected to attend* it."	*einberufen* · *man erwartet, daß ich teilnehme*
Second example: "What's that? Someone is *knocking* the door. There seems to be some kind of emergency. My God, he's *bleeding*. Goodbye."	*klopfen* · *bluten*
2. Invent technical *defects*	*Fehler*
You: Can you hear me alright? You *sound* very *faint*.	*klingen · schwach*
Chatterbox: Yes, I can hear you as *clear* as ...	*deutlich*
You: What did you say?	
Chatterbox: (*shouting*) I said I can hear you fine.	*brüllen*
You: What? You *can't* hear me *either*? I'll call you *right* back.	*können auch nicht* · *gleich*
Of course, you won't call them back and when your phone rings two minutes later, you don't answer it. This *confirms* that there is a *fault* on the line *at your end*.	*bestätigen* · *Fehler · bei Ihnen*

BOOKING A ROOM IN GLASGOW

CONTENTS

Our Telestory:	A pretty strong accent up there
Telefunctions:	Communication problems
Speech functions:	Booking a room
Your Teletrainer:	Let's practise speech and telefunctions
Teletiquette:	When not to call through your secretary
Your Teledoc:	Getting the feeling of the emotional caller
Our Telejokes:	Time for a smile

Time for a smile

Fred went to England on a business trip to buy books, tapes and films for his language courses. Every week he phoned up his fiancée:
"I'm awfully sorry, darling, but I think I've got to stay for another week. I'm still buying."
At the end of the sixth week, when he phoned again to make excuses, she said very coolly: "Come home at once darling, or I'll start selling what I think you're buying."

We speak a pretty strong accent up here

Andrew arrived in Glasgow after a long night. His secretary had forgotten to *book* a hotel. This is the third *attempt* to find a room.	*buchen* *Versuch*
Receptionist (**R**), Andrew Goodman (**A**)	
R: Hello, Penta Hotel, can I help you, sir?	
A: I *hope* you can. I'm calling to see if you've got a room for me.	*hoffen*
R: It's a bit difficult, sir. Just a moment, I'll *check* and ☛☆ ■ ❍ ➤ ✌ ✪.	*nachsehen*
A: What an accent! Could you speak more slowly please? Look, I'll take anything really. It's only for one night.	
R: Well, there is ✡ ❄ ❐ ✚ ☞.	
A: I beg your pardon but *I missed that.* Could you say that again, please?	*nicht verstehen*
R: ➜ ☆ ✭ ✪, if that's okay?	
A: Young lady, I'm sorry but could you speak *more clearly*. I didn't catch what you said.	*deutlicher*
R: Sorry, I know we have a pretty *strong accent* up here. I was talking to my colleague here, you know. Yes sir, we do have a small room with bathroom on the corridor.	*starker Akzent*
A: Okay. Well, could I reserve that please? I'll *be along in* twenty minutes.	*kommen*

Time for a smile

Fred phones to book a room for a week in a small town in Scotland. First he tries the cheapest[1] hotel. A woman answers the phone: "A single room for a week? Hm, we're booked out and short of staff[2]. Let me see ... Would you be ready to make your own bed[3], sir?" – "Yes, no problem". – "Then I'll give you our room number 13. In the little shed[4] in the yard[5] you will find hammer, nails and boards[6]."

1 das billigste 2 Personal 3 das Bett selber machen 4 Schuppen 5 Hof 6 Bretter

Telefunctions

Communication problems	
Could you speak more clearly / slowly, please?	Könnten Sie bitte deutlicher / langsamer sprechen?
I beg your pardon, but I missed that.	Entschuldigen Sie bitte, aber das habe ich nicht mitbekommen.
I'm not sure whether I got that right.	Ich weiß nicht, ob ich das richtig verstanden habe.
Could you say that again, please?	Könnten Sie das noch einmal wiederholen?
Could you repeat that, please?	Könnten Sie das bitte wiederholen?
Sorry, I know we have a pretty strong accent up here.	Tut mir leid, ich weiß, wir sprechen hier oben mit einem ziemlich starken Akzent.

Speech functions

Booking a room	Ein Zimmer reservieren
I'm phoning to reserve a room.	Ich rufe an, um ein Zimmer zu reservieren.
I'm calling to book a room.	Ich rufe an, um ein Zimmer zu bestellen.
I'm calling to see if you've got a room for me.	Ich rufe an, um zu fragen, ob Sie ein Zimmer für mich haben.
I'm just checking to see if you have any rooms free.	Ich wollte nur nachfragen, ob Sie Zimmer frei haben,
We're fully booked for that week, sir.	Wir sind in der Woche voll ausgebucht.
If you like, I could recommend another hotel.	Wenn Sie wünschen, könnte ich Ihnen ein anderes Hotel empfehlen.
I'm afraid I have to cancel my reservation for the 12th.	Ich muß meine Reservierung für den 12. leider stornieren.
Is it possible to change the booking?	Ist es möglich umzubuchen?

Your Teletrainer:

EXERCISE 1: Which functions are used in (almost) the same situation

1 *Sorry, I missed that.*	**a** *I beg your pardon, but you're speaking too fast for me.*
2 *Could you speak more slowly, please?*	**b** *The line is terrible.*
3 *We've got a bad connection.*	**c** *Could you speak up a bit, please?*
4 *Could you say that again, please?*	**d** *It's as if you were miles away.*
5 *Could you speak more loudly, please?*	**e** *Could you repeat that, please?*
6 *You sound very faint.*	**f** *I'm afraid, I didn't catch that.*

EXERCISE 2: Booking a room

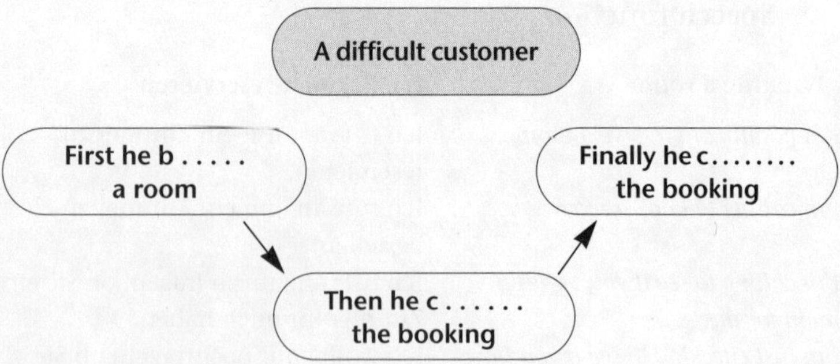

EXERCISE 3: Rearrange the conversation

1 *Hello, Penta Hotel, can I help you, sir?*
2 *How long would you like to stay?*
3 *Hm, we' re booked out and short of staff. Let me see.Would you be ready to make your own bed?*
4 *Yes, sir. I'll give you room number 13.*

a *Well. I would if it's necessary. Has it got a shower?*
b *Fine. I'll be along in 10 minutes.*
c *About a week. I'm here for the trade fair, you know.*
d *I hope you can. I'm phoning to book a room.*

EXERCISE 4: Spot Mimi's mistakes

*(**R**) Receptionist, (**M**) Mimi*

M: *Good day. I call you on to ask if you a room for me have.*
R: *Just a moment, I'll check. How many nights are you going to stay, madam?*
M: *Could you please slowlier talk? I am namely out Germany from the Waterkant, the wateredge how you Englander say.*
R: *How long are you going to stay – how many days?*
M: *It is for a night. How expensive is the room?*
R: *Well, we do have a small room, but without a shower. It's £ 12, including breakfast, of course.*
M: *Excuse you me, please. I have already again not understood. I believe I come better personally foreby. Tschüs.*
R: *Tschüs?? I'm afraid I didn't catch that. Are you still there?*

Teletiquette: When not to call through your secretary

If you are important enough, there are certain calls that you should dial personally rather than have your secretary do it:

1. If you want to flatter a person.
2. If you want to show respect and interest.

Your Teledoc:
Getting the feeling of the emotional caller

Mrs Anne Santer is neither a visual nor an auditive woman. She is the emotional one, the *kinesthetic type*. Now how do you find out on the phone that you have to do with a type like Mrs Anne Santer?

1. She speaks slowly on the phone.
2. She is not a woman of many words on the phone, because it is almost *impossible* for her to *express* feelings to someone she can neither see nor *trust*.
3. She is more interested in the way you speak to her than in what you have to say.
4. She might be a person who works with her hands and feet, a dancer, a doctor. She *prefers* sports she can feel: swimming, hiking and she likes *spicy* meals.
5. She will use words that describe what you can *touch* with your hands or feel on your *skin*: We can *handle* that; it feels like; I know how you feel about it; it smells a bit *fishy*; *grasp*, get in touch with, be under pressure; that gives me the *creeps*, *squeeze*, it goes under the skin; it was quite a shock for; *unbearable*; be confused; don't *lose* your head.

Pure types are *rare*, most people are a mixture of two or all three types. More about this in the next chapter.

Gefühlsmensch
unmöglich
ausdrücken
trauen
vorziehen
würzig
berühren · Haut
erledigen
verdächtig · greifen
Gänsehaut · ausquetschen
unerträglich
verlieren
selten

Time for a smile

The Health Minister[1], visiting a mental hospital[2], had difficulty[3] getting his telephone connection to London. Frustrated he shouted[4] to the operator, "Young lady, do you know who I am?" "No", was the calm reply, "but I do know where you are."

1 Gesundheitsminister 2 Irrenanstalt 3 Schwierigkeiten 4 schreien

DINNER FOR TWO

CONTENTS

Our Telestory:	**Trying to arrange dinner for two**
Speech functions:	**Making excuses**
Telefunctions:	**Last words on the phone**
Your Teletrainer:	**Let's practise excuses and last words**
Teletactics:	**How to avoid invitations**
Our Telejokes:	**Humorous stories around the phone**

Time for a smile

It happened[1] on the underground. On his way home from Tin Lizzy Ltd., Fred Niemec was mugged[2] and badly injured[3]. He woke up in hospital. The next day, his secretary was the first to phone him up.
"Now, Mr Niemec", she said, "don't worry about anything. We're all going to work together at the office to do your job – as soon as[4] we're able to find out what you've been doing."

1 passieren 2 ausrauben 3 verletzen 4 sobald

Trying to arrange dinner for two

Back to Fred Niemec. To *sign* the *contract* and *seal* the bargain, the Purchasing Manager at Hospital Services invited Fred to dinner. — *Vertrag unterzeichnen · besiegeln*

John Shark (**S**), Fred Niemec (**N**)

S: Hello, John Shark here. Excuse me for calling during your lunch break. Do you *remember* me? — *sich erinnern*

N: *I beg your pardon ...?* — *Wie bitte?*

S: Shark, John Shark. The Purchasing Director at Hospital Services.

N: Shark? ... Yes, I remember you. I'm so sorry, I didn't *recognise* your *voice*. I'm a little *overworked* at the moment, you know. — *erkennen · Stimme · überarbeitet*

S: I thought I'd give you a call, you know, to congratulate you formally on *winning the order*. It's not every day that we spend £ 150,000. We must have lunch some time. — *Auftrag erhalten*

N: Yes, we must. But first I'd like to *express* my *gratitude* and I wish you the best of luck with our automatic Tin Lizzy. — *ausdrücken · Dankbarkeit*

S: Listen, why don't we have dinner together to seal the *bargain*. You'd be my guest this time. When are you free? — *Geschäft*

N: I'm afraid I'll have to have a look in my *desk diary* first which unfortunately I don't have with me at the moment. — *Schreibtischkalender*

S: Desk diary? No *lame excuses*, Fred – I may call you Fred, mightn't I? I know a pizza place. It's in the centre of London. I'm just having a look in my pocket diary ... Let's say tomorrow, alright? — *faule Ausreden*

N: I wonder if you could *give me directions*. I don't know my way around the centre. — *Weg beschreiben*

S: Sure. Take the *underground* to James Street. When you come out ... — *U-Bahn*

N: Did you say underground? I'm not quite sure how to put this but I'm afraid I don't go by underground since I was *mugged* ... — *überfallen*

S: Another weak excuse, Fred. Bring along your multi-purpose lizzy to take care of *hooligans.* Go to James Street *tube station.* When you come out, cross Oxford Street, go along St. James Street and turn right at the end. It's the small pizza place on the *corner.* The owner might be a *potential customer* for your robots.	*Rowdies* / *U-Bahn-Station* / *an der Ecke* / *möglicher Kunde*
N: Really? Much *obliged* to you. Along St. James Street and turn left. Yes, what time?	*vielen Dank*
S: Shall we say 7 p.m.? I'm afraid I've got to go now. I have a meeting in five minutes. See you. Bye.	

Speech functions: Making excuses

Negatives ankündigen	
I'm afraid I've got to go now.	Ich muß leider Schluß machen.
I'm not quite sure how to put this, but I'm afraid that ...	Ich weiß nicht, wie ich es sagen soll, aber ich fürchte, daß ...

Der Partner weiß noch nicht, für was man sich entschuldigt	
Excuse me for not having called you back.	Entschuldigen Sie, daß ich nicht zurückgerufen habe.
Excuse me for calling during your lunch break, but ...	Entschuldigen Sie, daß ich Sie in Ihrer Mittagspause anrufe, aber ...

Entschuldigung bei Kommunikationsproblemen	
I beg your pardon ...?	Wie bitte ...?
I beg your pardon, I thought you were someone else.	Verzeihung. Ich dachte Sie wären jemand anderes.
I beg your pardon, I missed that.	Entschuldigen Sie, ich habe das nicht verstanden.

Bedauern während Pannen und Problemen	
I'm so sorry, I didn't recognise your voice.	Tut mir sehr leid, aber ich habe Ihre Stimme nicht erkannt.
I'm sorry to have kept you waiting.	Tut mir leid, daß ich Sie habe warten lassen.

Your Teletrainer

EXERCISE 1: Revision: Last words on the phone (see also chapter 1)

Don't end a call the abrupt way – add the reason why

I'm afraid I have to
- .. now.
- . . . this short.
- . . . this.

I have a meeting in five minutes.

I'm hard pressed for time.

I've got a full schedule.

Tell them that you enjoyed the telephone conversation

It's been nice ...
- ...... to you
- to h... from you
- h...... your voice again

Promise a conversation in a more relaxed atmosphere

Preparing the next call

- Keep in t....
- I'm looking f...... to hearing from you.
- I'll p.... you when I've more time.
- I'll g.. back to you soon.
- I'll r... you up again.
- You'll be h.....g f... me.

EXERCISE 2: Match excuse and reason

Excuse phrase		Reason
1	*Excuse me for*	a *Mr Brain isn't in.*
2	*I beg your pardon,*	b *I can't accept your invitation.*
3	*I'm sorry,*	c *not having called you back.*
4	*I'm afraid*	d *could you please repeat that?*

EXERCISE 3: Translation exercise

Verwenden Sie verschiedene Redewendungen der Entschuldigung.

S: John Shark am Apparat. Entschuldigen Sie, wenn ich in der Mittagspause anrufe. Sie erinnern sich an mich?
N: Verzeihung, wer ist am Apparat?
S: Shark, John Shark. Einkaufsleiter bei Hospital Services.
N: Shark? ... Ja natürlich erinnere ich mich an Sie. Entschuldigen Sie, aber ich habe Ihre Stimme nicht erkannt.
S: Ich möchte Sie zum Essen einladen. Wir könnten bei dieser Gelegenheit (on that occasion) unseren Vertrag unterschreiben.
N: Ich muß erst mal in meinem Terminkalender nachsehen. Leider habe ich ihn nicht bei mir.
S: Keine faulen Ausreden, Fred!

EXERCISE 4 : Lame excuses for you to complete

"Waiter, look at that: You've brought me a lobster[1] with only one claw[2]."
"I'm a . . . . . . s . . . . , sir, but it lost its claw in a fight."
"Never mind. Take it away and bring me the winner[3]."

Typist: This is Susan Smith, speaking. I'm not q . . . . s . . . how to . . . this, sir, but I'm a . . . . d I'll be late this morning. I've overslept[4].
Boss: You mean you sleep at home as well as in the office?

1 Hummer 2 Schere 3 Sieger 4 verschlafen

Teletactics: How to avoid invitations

Fred Niemec was not *delighted* when Shark *suggested* "We must have lunch some time". His *spontaneous* reaction "Yes, we must" was the only possible polite answer. If Mr Shark had any *sensitivity* at all, the conversation would have ended there and the subject of lunch would never be *mentioned* again.

entzückt · vorschlagen
spontan
Feingefühl
erwähnt

However, as you will have noticed, Mr Shark is not the *sensitive* type. And he is by no means an *exception*. He's the type of business man who will try to *talk you into* a date, a time and a place. If you don't find an excuse *immediately*, you will only have to *cancel* the appointment by phone or letter. Now here are a few *serious* and less serious *suggestions* what to answer to the following invitation:

feinfühlig
Ausnahme
überreden zu
sofort
absagen
ernst (gemeint)
Vorschläge

"I say, why don't we have dinner together to seal the *bargain*. You'd be my guest this time. When are you free?"

Geschäftsabschluß

- "When am I free? I'm afraid I'll have to have a look in my *master diary*, which I don't have with me at the moment." It's not difficult never to be in the same place as this *fictional* master diary.
- "But you must know that I'm a *vegetarian* and a *tea-totaller*. You will be my guest of course. I know a charming little *health-food restaurant* ...". Only useful if he or she is a *lover* of French *cuisine*.
- "Forgive me, but I'm not making any arrangements until I've finished the *diet* my doctors have *advised* me to keep."
- "I'm afraid I can't accept any invitation until my daughter has *returned* safely from her *Red Cross* mission in Bosnia."

Haupttermінkalender
erfunden
Vegetarier
Abstinenzler
Öko-Restaurant
Liebhaber
Küche
Diät
raten
zurückkehren · Rotes Kreuz

ANDREW SPREADS HIS WINGS

CONTENTS

Our Telestory:	Andrew turns down[1] an invitation and leaves for Germany
Your Teletrainer:	Mixed telefunctions
Your Teledoc:	Mirror the caller and win a friend
Our Telejokes:	Time for a smile

Time for a smile: Doing business in Scotland

In Glasgow, Andrew Goodman received a strange telephone call:
"McNab here. I'm calling to find out if your household robot could replace[2] a wife or a housemaid[3]. Please send me one of your robots and if it's good I'll send you a cheque."
"Well, Mr McNab", replied Andrew, "I'm very interested. But I suggest[4] that you send me your cheque and if it's good, I'll send you the robot."

1 ablehnen 2 ersetzen 3 Dienstmädchen 4 vorschlagen

An Invitation from Fussy

Reception (**R**), Fussy Pot (**F**), Andrew (**A**)

R: Hello, Penta Hotel, may I help you?

F: Yes, I'd like to speak to Andrew Goodman.

R: I'll just check if he's in *at present*. Yes, his key is not here, so he's in his room. I'll just put you through.

gegenwärtig

A: Hi, Andrew Goodman here.

F: Andy, it's me. I just wanted to know how it went with the robot. Did you sell one?

A: Sell one? I sold six of those little *metal men*. *Can you believe that*?

Metallmänner
kaum zu glauben

F: Wonderful! That's brilliant! And you're *on commission*, too!

Provision erhalten

A: Thanks for all your *support*. I'd never have done it without you.

Hilfe

F: How about a *celebration*? *It's on me*! I want *to take you out* for the night. When will you be here?

Feier · auf meine Rechnung
mit jemandem ausgehen

A: I'm arriving at the weekend. But I can only stay one day. The company is sending me to Germany. It seems they're interested in our robots. Okay, till later then, bye-bye.

F: Okay, take care till tomorrow, bye.

Andrew has to spread his wings

Andrew has signed his first contract, a deal of £500,000. He is at his desk at Robotalot when he gets a phone-call from the "big" boss.

Dr. Brain (**B**), Andrew Goodman (**A**)

A: Goodman here. Can I be of assistance?

B: Brain here. I'm pleased to get hold of you. I've been trying to get into contact with you for some time. Now, my boy, it's *in connection with* that business you did for the

es handelt sich um

company. I suppose I'm not the first, but I'd like to congratulate you *from the bottom of my heart*. Yours was the first we've sold.	von ganzem Herzen
A: Actually, we managed to sell six of them, sir. Let's hope the customer *remains satisfied*.	zufrieden bleiben
B: No doubt about that. Now *to the point*. I'm phoning because I want you to *spread your wings*. What about a *flight* to Germany? How do you feel about going international?	zur Sache flügge werden Flug
A: I didn't think of selling *abroad*, sir. I don't speak German, you know.	Ausland
B: My dear Goodman, mightn't it be an idea if you learnt the language? With your talents I'm sure that you'll *overcome* all *obstacles*. Now get the trip planned. We've booked you on an early flight tomorrow. *How time goes by*! Sorry, I can't talk to you now. I'll phone you when I have more time.	überwinden Hindernisse wie die Zeit verfliegt

Your Teletrainer

EXERCISE 1: Five steps to Andrew's hotel room

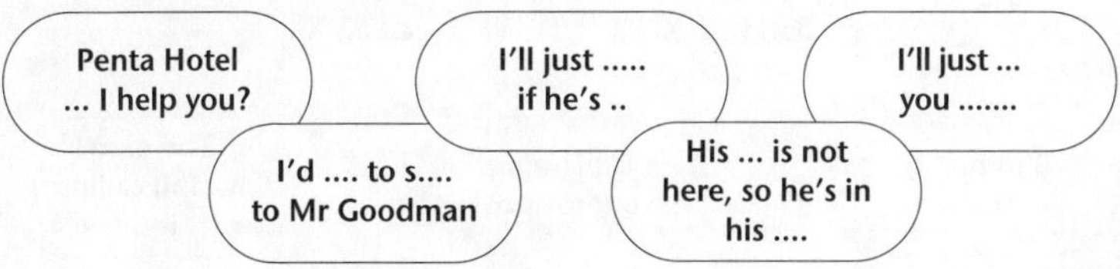

EXERCISE 2: Suggesting activities

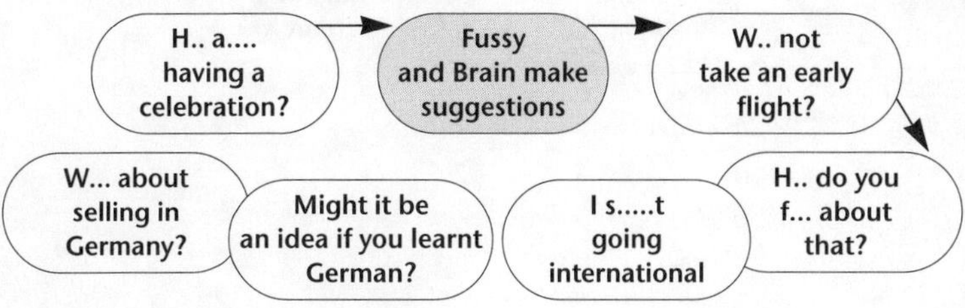

EXERCISE 3: How does Brain do it on the phone?

How does he...	
identify himself?	*Brain . . . .*
start the conversation?	*I'm pl . . . . . to g . . h . . . of you.*
say that he had tried before to get hold of Andrew?	*I've been tr . . . . to g . . i . c . . . . . t w . . . you for s . . e t . . e.*
introduce the purpose of his call?	*It's in c . . . . w . . . X.*
introduce his purpose again?	*Now to the p . . . . I'm p . . . . . g b . . . . . e...*
end the call?	*I can't t . . . to you n . . .*
say that he will call later?	*I'll p . . . . you when I have m . . . t . . .*

EXERCISE 4: More telephone power

Explaining your purpose

It's in c.....ion with X

It c......s X

I'm p.....g b.....e

The r....n w.. I'm calling is ...

I'm c.....g to ask ...

I'm r.....g about X

Your Teledoc: Mirror the caller and win a friend

Why is it important to be able to *recognize* the auditive, visual and emotional callers? Well, you can use your knowledge to win their *trust.* And if they trust you, you will find it easier to do business with them.

erkennen · *Vertrauen*

How is it done?

Be their *mirror,* as far as language *is concerned.* Since you know the *linguistic preferences* of the three types of callers:

Spiegel · betreffen · *sprachliche Vorliebe*

- Use the vocabulary of the visual caller, and he or she will *see eye to eye* with you. *sich verstehen*
- *Adopt* the vocabulary of auditive callers and they will listen to you for longer than they had originally planned. *übernehmen*
- *Tune in* to the emotional caller and he will *feel at home* with you. *einstimmen* · *sich zu Hause fühlen*

There is more you can do:

- *Adapt* your tempo of speaking to the caller's *speed*. He/she will understand you better. *anpassen* · *Geschwindigkeit*
- Don't speak louder than the person you are talking to.
- *Avoid* dialect if the caller speaks Hochdeutsch or standard English. *vermeiden*

And now the most important *piece of advice*: Don't *exaggerate.* Remain natural. Test yourself and *record* your conversations *on tape.*

Ratschlag · *übertreiben* · *auf Band aufnehmen*

Just in case[1] you would like to order a robot

Both of our dynamic salesmen have their meetings with potential customers. What happened in the two meetings is not our business. In general we can say: They both signed contracts. Of course the two salesmen are very happy. They've both achieved[2] something.
Here are their brand new business cards[3] in case you want to order[4] a robot for your family.

Andrew Goodman
Salesman at

ROBOTALOT

56–64 Albert Road
Tottenham · London TN 126
Tel.: 01 263 1226
Fax: 01 263 1230

Fred Niemec

TIN LIZZY, Ltd
Salesteam

1–3 Burton Road
Hemstead · London WC
Tel.: 01 262 34970

1 für den Fall, daß 2 etwas erreichen 3 Visitenkarte 4 bestellen

ROBOT OR FUSSY - THAT IS THE QUESTION

CONTENTS

Our Telestory:	Get off the phone!
Telefunctions:	Getting angry on the phone
Speech functions:	Rearranging appointments
Your Teletrainer	Let's practise speech and telefunctions
Our Telejokes:	Time for a smile

Time for a smile

After a hard day's work Andrew phones up his fiancée, Fussy, to arrange a date and celebrate[1] their anniversary[2]:

Andrew: Fussy, I'll love you forever. When can we get together. Suggest[3] the time and the place. I would climb the highest mountain for you; I would swim the widest river for you, I would ...

Fussy: Oh Andy, I love you, too, come to my house now ... quick.

Andrew: OK, as soon as it stops raining.

1 feiern 2 Jahrestag ihrer Bekanntschaft 3 vorschlagen

Get off the phone!

So Andrew will *have to* go to Germany, the world's marketplace. But first he has a difficult phone-call to answer.	*muß*
Secretary (**S**), Fussy Pot (**F**), Andrew (**A**)	
S: I'm afraid I can't put you through, Miss Pot. Mr Goodman is in a *meeting*. They're having trouble with this robot, you know. I suggest you try again tomorrow.	*Besprechung*
F: And I advise you to put me through *immediately* or Mr Goodman and his robot will be in real trouble.	*sofort*
S: But he left strict *instructions* that he was not to be *disturbed*.	*Anweisungen* *stören*
F: Mr Goodman will be very angry if you don't put me through to him. It's in his interest and in the *interest* of the company.	*Interesse*
S: Please *calm down!* I'm only doing my job. Well, if you *insist* ... Mr Goodman's phone is ringing for you.	*sich beruhigen* *bestehen auf*
F: Hi there, Andrew, how is my *successful* salesman?	*erfolgreich*
A: Oh, not bad, thanks.	
F: You don't *sound* very sure. Listen Andrew, I'm really *looking forward* to our long weekend. It's our *anniversary*, you know.	*klingen* *sich freuen* *Jahrestag*
A: Yes, I know. Listen, I'm afraid that *I can't make it* this weekend. Couldn't we *postpone* this anniversary?	*ich schaffe es nicht* *verschieben*
F: What did you say? This weekend is our anniversary! That has *priority* over everything. What's this all about now?	*Vorrang*
A: Listen, Fussy. The boss phoned me five minutes ago. He wants me to go to Germany tomorrow. Let's *fix* another date.	*vereinbaren*
F: Oh, that's typical of you. You've had this job	

for five minutes and your robot is already more important than me. Look, *get off the phone!* I've had enough of this!	*leg auf, geh aus der Leitung!*

Telefunctions: Getting angry on the phone

Getting angry	**Ärgerlich werden**
I want to speak to your boss personally. It's in his interest, not mine.	Ich möchte Ihren Chef persönlich sprechen. Es ist in seinem, nicht in meinem Interesse.
Mr Goodman will be very angry if you don't put me through to him immediately.	Herr Goodman wird sehr ärgerlich sein, wenn Sie mich nicht sofort mit ihm verbinden.
I advise you to put me through now or I'll cancel the order with your company.	Ich rate Ihnen, mich jetzt zu verbinden, oder ich storniere den Auftrag für Ihre Firma.
I know that Mr Brain is in. I was on the phone to him five minutes ago.	Ich weiß, daß Herr Brain da ist. Ich habe vor fünf Minuten mit ihm telefoniert.
Could you give me your name, please? I'm going to complain about you.	Würden Sie mir bitte Ihren Namen sagen? Ich werde mich über Sie beschweren.
This is a long-distance call. I can't hold any longer.	Dies ist ein Ferngespräch. Ich kann nicht länger warten.

What to say to the angry caller	**Was man dem verärgerten Anrufer sagt**
Please be patient. It won't take long.	Haben Sie Geduld. Es dauert nicht lange.
Please calm down! I'm doing my best.	Bitte beruhigen Sie sich. Ich tue mein Bestes.
I'm only doing my job.	Ich tue nur meine Pflicht.
I suggest you try again tomorrow.	Ich schlage vor, Sie versuchen es morgen noch einmal.

Speech functions: Rearranging appointments

Cancelling appointments	**Termine absagen**
I'm afraid I can't make it.	Ich fürchte, ich schaffe es nicht.
I'm afraid I've got to cancel our appointment.	Ich muß unseren Termin leider absagen.
I won't be able to keep the appointment we made.	Ich kann den Termin für unser Treffen nicht einhalten.
Something unexpected has happened.	Etwas Unerwartetes ist passiert.

My secretary, who manages my agenda, didn't know that ...	**Meine Sekretärin, die meinen Terminkalender führt, wußte nicht, daß ...**
... I'm booked up that afternoon.	... ich an dem Nachmittag voll ausgebucht bin.
... I had got something scheduled for then.	... ich schon etwas eingeplant hatte.
... I would be tied up on that Monday	... ich an dem Montag keine Zeit haben würde.

Rearranging appointments	**Termine ändern**
Could we fix another appointment?	Könnten wir einen anderen Termin vereinbaren?
Let's fix another date then.	Machen wir eben einen anderen Termin aus.
Would it be possible to postpone our meeting?	Wäre es möglich, unseren Termin zu verschieben?
I hope I haven't messed up your arrangements too much.	Ich hoffe, ich habe Ihre Termine nicht zu sehr durcheinandergebracht.

Time for a smile

A police officer was talking to the chief of police over the phone: "A man has been robbed down here, and I've got one of them. What shall I do?" – "Which one have you got?" asked the chief. –"The one who was robbed", the officer replied.

Your Teletrainer

EXERCISE 1: Let's have a second look at the telephone conversation and practise the functions

Was sie hätten sagen können	Was die Personen gesagt haben
	The Secretary
I'm afraid I can't connect you.	*I'm afraid I ....*
Why don't you try again tomorrow?	*I .... you try again tomorrow.*
I've been told not to disturb him.	*He has .... not to be disturbed.*
Don't get excited.	*Please ....*
I'm putting you through now.	*His p.... .. r...... for you.*
	Fussy Pot
You'd better connect me at once.	*I a...... you .. ... me ...... i.........*
I've got to to cut this short.	*... ... the phone!*
I'm glad that we are meeting at the weekend.	*I'm .... to our weekend.*
	Andrew Goodman
I have to cancel our appointment.	*I ...'. .... it.*
Could we fix another day for our anniversary?	*Couldn't we .... this anniversary?*
We'd better fix another day.	*...'. fix another date then.*

Time for a smile

Fussy was staying at an expensive[1] hotel. She wanted to have breakfast in bed. So she studied the menu[2] and phoned room service[3] and ordered a large English breakfast.
"And for dessert, I'll have Pascuale Casanova." she said.
"I beg you pardon? What did you say you wanted for dessert?" asked the bewildered[4] head waiter.
"I'll try your Pascuale Casanova." "I'm afraid, madam," replied the waiter, "that is out of the question. Mr Casanova is our director."

1 teuer 2 Speisenkarte 3 Zimmerservice 4 verwirrt

EXERCISE 2: What to say when you're getting impatient

- I've been h...... for a..s
- You p...... me through to the wrong de.......t
- You gave me the wrong e.......n
- I can't h.l. any l.n..r
- Listen, operator! I'm losing patience...

EXERCISE 3: Correct Mimi's English

M: *I am the Mimi out Aurich. I want from you a roboter buy. Bandage me please with the director. You must know, this is a fartalk out Aurich. Make you it not so long.*

R: *I'm afraid our director is not available at the moment. Can I be of assistance?*

M: *Much light you can that. I will know if your roboter also my cat feed can and with her play can? But my Pussy is a very wild and great cat, must you know.*

R: *Our model Z – Z stands for zoo – is programmed to feed tigers and to keep lions happy. If it can feed a tiger, it can feed Pussy.*

EXERCISE 4: Speaking to the impatient caller

- I can't hold any longer
- Please, be p.....t, it won't take long
- I'm going to complain about you
- I'm only d...g my j..
- Why can't you put me through?
- I'm d...g my b..t
- Please c..m d..n

HEADING FOR THE CENTRE OF THE WORLD

CONTENTS

Our Telestory:	Confirming an appointment in Germany
Telefunctions:	Ending a call and thanking the caller
Your Teletrainer:	Let's practise starters and stoppers
Telefunctions:	Private calls
Telejokes:	Time for smile

Time for a smile

Mr Slicer was sitting in his office when the telephone rang. Fred Niemec was on the line:
"Listen carefully, sir. I've got to read you an important message from Mr Shark, a potential customer for our Tin Lizzy."
"Go ahead and read it. Be quick, I haven't got any time to waste[1]," said Slicer.
"Well, my secretary will read it. She's got a lovely voice among other perfections[2]."
So the secretary began: "Interested in Lizzy ... stop ... price still too high ... stop ... order ten ... stop ... fifteen percent discount ... stop..." – "Niemec!!" roared[3] Slicer over the phone, "leave the girl alone and let her read the telegram. This is business!"

1 Zeit verschwenden 2 Vorzüge 3 brüllen

Confirming an appointment in Germany

Andrew Goodman, *though* depressed about Fussy's reaction, decides *to put* his work *first*. Indeed he is quite motivated. The German company might be an important customer. They are specialised in *catering for* industry: office cleaning, cooking etc. *Chance will have* it that Mimi from Aurich in East-Frisia works in that company as a receptionist.

obwohl
Vorrang geben
beliefern
Wie der Zufall es will ...

Mimi (**M**), Andrew (**A**), Herr Geiger (**G**)

M: Industry Services GmbH. Mimi Salkes am Apparat.

A: Oh sorry, I didn't catch what you said. I don't speak German. Do you speak English?

M: *Naturally, and very good.

** typical Teutonic English*

A: Yes, I can hear that. Well, my name's Goodman. I'm coming to your company to see your *purchasing manager*. Could you put me through to his *department*, please?

Einkaufsleiter
Abteilung

M: *Mean you Herrn Geiger?

A: I don't actually know his name.

M: *When you his name not know how can you a date have?

A: Listen, young lady, the *appointment* was arranged for me. Could you *transfer* me, please?

Verabredung
verbinden

M: *I'm bandaging you now.

G: Helmut Geiger am Apparat.

A: Hello, my name's Goodman from Robotalot in England. It's *in connection with* some robots for your company. I think you asked for a *quotation* and a demonstration.

es geht um
Angebot

G: That's right, Mr Goodman. How do you do? We've been waiting for your call.

A: Fine, thanks. I had some *trouble* getting through to you. The receptionist didn't seem to know anything.

Probleme

G: Oh, that's *staff* nowadays in Germany. Many of them cost a *fortune*, do nothing, and think they know everything. It's a *sign of the times.*	*Personal* *Vermögen* *Zeichen der Zeit*
A: Well, I'll be flying in on the 26th. I think we're meeting at 11:30.	
G: That's in two days. The *entire* company is curious to see the *miracles* your robot will *perform.*	*ganze* *Wunder · vollbringen*
A: Me too! Could you possibly give me a few directions. From the airport.	
G: It's very easy if you take the Lufthansa bus. It brings you directly to the centre. Then take a taxi; it's only two minutes.	
A: Right. What's the exact address?	
G: It's Römerstraße 21, 69115 Heidelberg.	
A: What's the number, please?	
G: Actually I told you. It's 21.	
A: Oh I see! The rest is the *postal code* of Heidelberg. Could you *spell out* the street, please. I didn't get it.	*Postleitzahl* *buchstabieren*
G: Of course. R – O with two *dots* on it – M – E – R – Strasse. Number 21 in Heidelberg. *Anything else* I can do for you?	*Punkte* *Sonst noch etwas?*
A: Okay. I think that's it for now. Well, thank you very much for your help. You'll be hearing from me.	
G: Thanks for ringing. So long!	

Time for a smile

An American and a British shoe salesman travelled on the same boat to West Africa, each representing[1] different shoe companies. After landing they looked around, and what struck[2] them first was that all the natives[3] were barefoot[4]. The British salesman cabled[5] his head office: "Nobody here wearing shoes. Coming home by next ship." The American salesman cabled his chief: "Nobody here wearing shoes. Market wide open[6]."

1 vertreten 2 auffallen 3 Eingeborene 4 barfuß 5 telegraphieren 6 ein großer Markt

Telefunctions: Ending a call and thanking the caller

Signalling the end	**Gesprächsende signalisieren**
Anything else I can do for you?	Kann ich sonst noch etwas für Sie tun?
Will there be anything else?	Gibt es sonst noch etwas (zu besprechen)?
I think that's it for now.	Ich glaube, das wär's einstweilen.

Thanking the caller	**Dem Anrufer danken**
Thanks for ringing.	Vielen Dank, daß Sie angerufen haben.
Thank-you for calling.	Vielen Dank für Ihren Anruf.
Thank-you for the call.	Vielen Dank für Ihren Anruf.

Saying goodbye	**Sich verabschieden**
Goodbye for now.	Auf Wiederhören einstweilen.
Goodbye then.	Also, auf Wiederhören.
Bye then.	Wiederhören.
Bye.	Wiederhören.
Cheers.	Tschüß. / Danke.
See you.	Bis bald.
So long.	Bis zum nächsten Mal.

Your Teletrainer

EXERCISE 1: Look at the dialogue again and correct Mimi's English

Naturally, and very good.
Mean you Herrn Geiger?
When you his name not know
how can you a date have?

EXERCISE 2: Let's expand it

B . .

B . . t . . . .

Goodbye . . . n.

Goodbye f . . n . .

EXERCISE 3: A second look at the conversation

Wenn es so nicht gesagt wurde ...	... wie wurde es dann gesagt?
I didn't get that.	*I didn't c . . . . what you s . . . .*
Could you connect me?	*Could you p . . me t . . . . . . ?*
Could you put me through?	*Could you tr . . . . . r me?*
It is about the robot.	*It's in co . . . . with the robot.*
I've been looking forward to your call.	*We've been w . . . . .g for your call.*
Will there be anything else?	*Anything else I c . . . d . . . . you?*
I'll get back to you soon.	*You'll be h . . . . . . from me.*

Telefunctions: Private calls

Identifying the caller	
Who's speaking?	Wer ist am Apparat?
Who's that/there?	Wer ist am Apparat?
Who am I speaking to?	Mit wem spreche ich?
Is that you, Tom?	Bist du's, Tom?

Polite noises	
I hope I'm not disturbing you.	Ich hoffe, ich störe dich nicht.
Not at all.	Keineswegs, nicht im geringsten.
What's the matter?	Was gibt es? Um was geht es?
I wonder/was wondering if you can spare me a minute ...?	Hast Du vielleicht einen Moment Zeit (für mich) ...?
... or shall I call back later?	... oder soll ich später noch einmal anrufen?

EXERCISE 4: Let's have a second look at private calls

Fred Niemec phoned his friend who was a doctor.	
*Fred Niemec (**F**), His doctor friend (**D**)*	
F: *This is Fred Niemec speaking. I wonder if you can . . . . . **me a m** . . . . . .?*	eine Minute Zeit haben
D: *Hello Fred, I haven't heard from you . . . .*	seit einer Ewigkeit
How are you? What's the matter?	
F: *Well, Charles, I don' t know how to put it, but I' m afraid my sex-life **isn't what it used to be.***	ist nicht mehr so, wie es einmal war
D: *Well, Fred, I **suppose** you have been working*	vermuten
*too hard for months. Get **some exercise.** Try*	sich Bewegung machen
***riding a bike** a few miles every day.*	radfahren
(Four days later)	
F: *Good evening, Charles. It's Fred a . . . . . I hope I'm **n . . d** . . . . **you.***	stören
D: *Not at . . . . Has your sex life **improved**?*	keineswegs · sich bessern
F: *How would I know? I'm seventy miles from home **by now**.*	inzwischen

STRAIGHT INTO THE LION'S DEN

CONTENTS

Our Telestory:	**Niemec to the centre of the world**
Telefunctions:	**Having technical problems**
Your Teletrainer:	**Make them speak up**
Speech functions:	**Praising people**
Your Teledoc:	**Don't interrupt – encourage**
Teletiquette:	**Telephone culture and time management**
Our Telejokes:	**Time for a smile**

Time for a smile

Every time Andrew checks into a hotel, he casually[1] tells the operator[2] to get the White House or 10 Downing Street on the phone. Then he asks to speak to the President or the Prime-minister. "I never get them on the phone," he tells his friends, "but from then on, I'm always sure to receive[3] great service at the hotel."

1 lässig 2 Vermittlung 3 erhalten, bekommen

Niemec to the centre of the world

So Andrew is off to the centre of the world: Germany. Mr Slicer, meanwhile the Marketing Director of Tin Lizzy, has heard about this potential customer in Germany. He *contacts* Industry Services and gets an *appointment* for Fred Niemec, too. He phones Fred.	*anrufen* · *Termin*
Marketing Director Mr Slicer (**S**), Fred (**F**)	
S: Hello, Slicer here. Can you hear me? The *line* is very bad. Am I speaking to Niemec?	*Verbindung*
F: Who is there? Could you speak up a bit? You *sound very faint*.	*leise klingen*
S: We've got *a crossed line*, I suppose. Can you hear me now? Slicer here. Is that you, Niemec?	*jemanden in der Leitung haben*
F: Oh, Mr Slicer. The *connection* is too bad. You'd better try again. (after five minutes)	*Verbindung*
S: This is Slicer speaking. What the hell was wrong with your phone, Niemec?	
F: Good afternoon, Mr Slicer. I hope you can hear me alright now. *Anything wrong* with our Tin Lizzy?	*etwas nicht in Ordnung?*
S: Not at all. We've all heard how well you did with Tin Lizzy I. May I take the *opportunity* to compliment you on your *achievement* ...	*Gelegenheit* · *Leistung*
F: Thank you very much.	
S: Let me come *to the point*. A man of your *success* and motivation should go *straight* into *the lion's den* – to Germany.	*zur Sache* · *Erfolg* · *direkt* · *Höhle des Löwen*
F: Oh, Mr Slicer. I can't speak German. I don't know the market.	
S: Nonsense! You speak English. They do, too, some sort of English. And if you can sell yourself, you can sell anything. Now listen,	

it's a *service* company for industry. They offer *cleaning* and cooking. So offer Tin Lizzy.	*Dienstleistungs-* *Reinigung*
F: But, sir, the robot doesn't have functions for *kitchen work.*	*Küchenarbeit*
S: Nonsense, what *difference* is there between kitchen and cleaning? Shouldn't a kitchen be clean? *There you are*! Now get your *arrangements* made and go and SELL, SELL, SELL!	*Unterschied* *Na also!* · *Vorbereitungen*
F: I'm afraid I need a few details about this company. Mr Slicer! Mr Sli... He has hung up on me! No information, no goodbye, nothing. What a company!	

Telefunctions: Having technical problems

What to say if the line is bad	
We've got a crossed line.	Das ist jemand in der Leitung.
I can't hear you very well.	Ich kann Sie nicht gut verstehen.
I can't hear you very distinctly.	Ich kann dich nicht deutlich hören.
I can hardly hear you.	Ich kann Sie kaum verstehen.
I can hardly hear your voice.	Ich kann Ihre Stimme kaum hören.
I can't make out what you're saying.	Ich kann nicht verstehen, was Sie sagen.
It's as if you're miles away.	Es klingt, als wären Sie meilenweit weg.
You sound very faint.	Sie klingen sehr leise.
There's an awful noise here.	Hier ist ein fürchterlicher Lärm.
The line is terrible.	Die Verbindung ist furchtbar schlecht.
The line is very bad. I hope you can hear me properly.	Die Leitung ist sehr schlecht. Ich hoffe, Sie können mich gut verstehen.
We've got a bad connection.	Wir haben eine sehr schlechte Verbindung.
There's terrible interference.	Da ist ein schreckliches Nebengeräusch.

How to make them speak up	
Could you speak louder, please?	Könnten Sie bitte lauter sprechen?
Could you speak up, please?	Könnten Sie bitte lauter sprechen?
Could you speak more clearly / slowly, please?	Könnten Sie bitte deutlicher / langsamer sprechen?
Would you please repeat the last remark?	Würden Sie die letzten Worte bitte wiederholen?
Sorry, I didn't quite catch that.	Tut mir leid, das habe ich nicht mitbekommen.

Your Teletrainer

EXERCISE 1: The Quality of Lines

c . . . . . d

t . . . . . le | **Lines can be** | **a . . . l**

b . .

EXERCISE 2: Complete the joke

McTavish was short of cash[1] so he ph . . . . up his friend, McNab, and asked for a loan[2] of ten pounds.
"Sorry," said McNab, "you'll have to s . . . . . . , I can't . . . . a . . . . you're saying".
"Can you lend[3] me ten pounds?" screamed[4] McTavish into the phone.
"Look," said McNab, "the . . . . is t . . . . , I can't m . . . o . . what you're saying."
At this stage the operator[5] chipped[6] in and said, "There's nothing wrong with the line, I can hear the caller d . . . ."
"In that case[7], why don't you lend him the ten pounds?" cried McNab.

1 knapp bei Kasse 2 Kredit 3 leihen 4 schreien 5 Vermittlung 6 in die Leitung gehen 7 in diesem Fall

EXERCISE 3: Communication problems

- **Sometimes you can't**
- hear him w . . .
- u . . . . d a word
- hear his v . . . .
- . . . . out what she says
- hear her cl . . .ly
- hear what he s . . s

EXERCISE 4: Complete the compliments

New secretary:	*I've . . . . about your business skills.*
Director (pleased):	*Oh, really. Well it's not worth talking about.*
New secretary:	*Yes, that's what I've heard.*

Boss to his new salesman:
We would like to c . . . . nt . . . . . your work – but when are you going to do any?

Speech functions: Praising employees

I'd like to congratulate you on...	Ich möchte Ihnen gratulieren zu...
I'd like to compliment you on...	Ich muß Ihnen ein Kompliment machen...
That was really good!	Das war wirklich gut.
Well done! That was a marvellous performance.	Gut gemacht! Das war eine hervorragende Leistung.
You surprised us all.	Sie haben uns alle überrascht.
I've heard a lot about you.	Ich habe viel von Ihnen gehört.
I'd like to take the opportunity to compliment you on your work.	Ich möchte die Gelegenheit nutzen, um Ihnen ein Kompliment für Ihre Arbeit zu machen

Your Teledoc: Don't interrupt – encourage

Andrew Goodman is a *skilled* listener on the phone. He knows when to *interrupt* and when to listen. He *encourages* the caller to go on talking in order to win time to understand a problem more fully and to analyse his or her personality.

geübt
unterbrechen
ermutigen

You do this by listening actively. Listen actively means *providing* feedback to the speaker. Thus you *exert* some *influence* over future *messages*, over what might or might not be said. How is this done on the phone? By words, of course. Here are five categories of very simple *speech functions* that encourage callers to go on talking and help you to learn more about them.

geben
beeinflussen
Botschaft
Redemittel

1. *Moderate praise*: That's not bad! Not bad at all!
2. Showing interest: Oh! How interesting! How *extraordinary*!
3. Showing *astonishment*: Well, well, well!

gemäßigtes Lob
außergewöhnlich
Erstaunen

Fancy that! You don't say! Would you believe it? *Incredible*!	*unglaublich*
4. Question tags are a typical British way to *accompany* a caller's story: René has given up drinking – *He hasn't, has he?* He's going to marry next week. – *He isn't, is he*? He met Schneider last week. *He didn't, did he*?	*begleiten*
5. *Agreeing and disagreeing*: Quite true. Quite right. I think so, too. I see your point. Absolutely! Definitely! Is that so? Really? Are you sure? I wonder? Who knows?	*einer Meinung und anderer Meinung sein*
In the absence of eye contact and body language, these speech functions might avoid *embarrassing silences* on the phone. They give you and your caller time to think and to formulate the message *accurately*. And what is more important – you win time to analyse the caller.	*ohne*; *peinliches Schweigen*; *genau*

Time for a smile

One director to the other: "I've heard so much about you. Now, I'd like to hear your side of the story."

The doctor's phone rang in the middle of the night.
"Doctor! This is Mr Williams of 88 London Road. My wife has terrible pains. Can you come to see her straight away[1], please? I think she's got appendicitis[2]."
"That's impossible, Mr Williams. Your wife had her appendix[3] out last year. Have you ever heard of anyone having a second appendix?"
"No, doctor", said Mr Williams, "but have you ever heard of anyone having a second wife?"

1 umgehend, sofort 2 Blinddarmentzündung 3 Blinddarm

Teletiquette: Telephone culture and time management

You want to call ... let us say, Mrs Armbruster. She's *chairperson* of Lepo Cars Ltd., one of your biggest clients. You have to talk to her personally about a *matter* of some *importance*. Here is what you might do:

Vorstandsvorsitzende
Angelegenheit · Wichtigkeit

- Phone up her secretary and ask when Mrs Armbruster would have the *necessary* time free for an *uninterrupted* discussion.
- *Describe* the kind of information you need, so she can have it *to hand* when you call back.

notwendig
ohne Unterbrechung
beschreiben
parat

Supposing Mrs Armbruster needed important information from you. She would have enough telephone culture to give you *advance warning* so that you can *set aside* the time, and will be able to give you her undivided *attention*. You *owe* it to yourself and to Mrs Armbruster to be *prepared*. It would make a very bad *impression* on Mrs Armbruster if you had to call for your secretary, or run across the office and *rummage* in the *drawers* of your *desk* while Mrs Armbruster is on the line.

angenommen
Vorankündigung
reservieren
Aufmerksamkeit
schulden
vorbereitet · Eindruck
wühlen · Schublade · Schreibtisch

Let's suppose you know that whenever Mrs Armbruster picks up the phone it's going to be a *lengthy* call. And let's suppose you are hard pressed for time. In that case you should inform the lady as early as possible telling her how long you can talk and give her the *option* to call back at an *agreed hour*.

langwierig
Wahl
vereinbarte Zeit

ROBOTS TO GERMANY

CONTENTS

Our Telestory:	**Two successful salesmen**
Telefunctions:	**Impatience on the phone**
Your Teletrainer:	**Increase your wordpower**
Teletiquette:	**Where "Handies[1]" don't come in handy**
Our Telejokes:	**Time for a smile**

Time for a smile

In this chapter Robotalot is going to make a big profit. So Dr. Brain can have his office redecorated[2] and furnished[3]. His favourite item[4] is a telephone receiver[5] made of gold. Right away, on the first day, Jane Simpson announced: "A client would like to speak to you." "Ask him to come in, " replied Dr. Brain. And to impress[6] his client he walked quickly to his desk and put the golden receiver to his ear: "Yes, yes, sir, of course. So long!" The visitor was impressed. "And what can I do for you?" asked Dr. Brain, slowly putting down the golden receiver. "I, eh, I, er, hm ... I would like to connect[7] your telephone, sir."

1 Achtung! "Handy" gibt es im Englischen nicht, man sagt "cellphone" oder "portable"
2 renovieren 3 möblieren 4 Lieblingsgegenstand 5 Hörer 6 beeindrucken 7 anschließen

Andrew Goodman has got the contract

The contract contract with Industry Services in his pocket Andrew goes back to his hotel. He has only just sat down when he *receives* a phone-call from Robotalot.	*erhalten*
Dr. Brain (**B**), Andrew Goodman (**A**)	
B: Brain here. Is that you Goodman?	
A: Yes, Goodman speaking. Who am I speaking to?	
B: It's me, Brain. Your employer. Didn't you *recognise* my voice?	*erkennen*
A: Sorry sir, no I didn't. We've got a bad connection.	
B: Bad connection in Germany? *What's the world coming to?* Now tell me what happened at the meeting?	*Wo soll das enden?*
A: It went alright, sir. We got the *contract.*	*Vertrag*
B: I say, well done, my boy. I knew you had it in you. What about *terms*?	*Bedingungen*
A: Well, we've sold three robots, *executive version*, selling price $ 250,000 per robot. *Delivery* of all three by December 15th of this year.	*Luxusmodell* · *Lieferung*
B: You lowered the price ... but it's okay as a *launch price* on the German market. But the delivery date is very, very *close.* What about functions?	*Einführungspreis* · *eng*
A: Well, I was quite open about the fact that the robot could only do certain things. I didn't *pretend* it could *cover* all situations. So they'll use it in the kitchens of their company and for office cleaning at their customers. They seemed to *accept* that.	*vortäuschen* · *abdecken* · *akzeptieren*
B: I can only congratulate you once again, my boy. Well, I'll have to say goodbye now. You'll give me a ring when you get back, won't you? Well, so long. Take care.	

Fred Niemec is on his mobile phone

We see Fred sitting in a restaurant; while waiting for his steak, he takes out his *portable* and phones Tin Lizzy, Ltd.	*Handy*
Mr Slicer (**S**), Fred Niemec (**N**)	
S: Hello, Slicer speaking. Is that you Niemec?	
N: Yes, it is, Mr Slicer.	
S: Well, what sort of contract did you manage to sign? What are the details?	
N: Oh, it was quite successful, Mr Slicer.	
S: Come on man, tell me the *details*! I haven't got all day.	*Einzelheiten*
N: What do you want to know?	
S: Listen, this is a *long-distance call*. I can't keep waiting for ever. *Fire away*, man!	*Ferngespräch* *schießen Sie los*
N: Well, I sold one robot, our *"super-cheapy"*. The price was fixed at $ 100,000.	*Billigstausführung*
S: My goodness, Niemec. That's almost giving it away. We can't produce it so cheap. Oh, well too late. What about the *delivery date*.	*Liefertermin*
N: Six weeks!	
S: We'll need a *miracle*!	*Wunder*
N: And I *promised* them it had functions to deal with office cleaning, cooking and also re...	*versprechen*
S: That can't be true. Only one or two functions are *foolproof* and certainly not those you *mentioned*. Well, I don't know where this will all *lead* us. I'd like to learn more about this contract. But not now. I've got this *suspicious* guy from the bank waiting outside.	*idiotensicher* *erwähnen* *hinführen* *mißtrauisch*
N: When would be a good time to call you back?	
S: Let's say in the afternoon. I will be at my club. You can *page* me there and I'll get back to you *immediately*. Well, bye for now. Keep in touch.	*anpiepsen* *sofort*

Telefunctions

Impatience on the phone	**Ungeduld am Telefon**
I haven't got all day.	Ich habe nicht den ganzen Tag Zeit.
I can't keep waiting for ever	Ich kann nicht ewig warten.
Operator, I've been holding on for ages.	Vermittlung, ich warte nun schon eine Ewigkeit.
This is a long-distance call. I can't hold on any longer.	Dies ist ein Ferngespräch. Ich kann nicht länger warten.
This is the second time you have passed me on to the wrong department.	Dies ist nun schon das zweite Mal, daß Sie mir die falsche Abteilung gegeben haben.
I get cut off every time I dial Mr Brain's number.	Ich werde jedesmal unterbrochen, wenn ich Herrn Brains Nummer wähle.
What do I have to do to get you to put me through – wait till Christmas?	Was muß ich noch tun, damit Sie mich verbinden – soll ich etwa bis Weihnachten warten?

Time for smile

When the Vatican got into financial trouble[1] after the Ambrosio Bank scandal, a rich Italian wine producer[2] thought that his day had come[3]. He phoned the Pope:
"Your Holiness, I'm calling to offer you a good bargain[4]. I'll balance your budget[5] if your Holiness would modify[6] one line in the Lord's Prayer[7]."
"Which line are you referring[8] to, my son?", asked the Pope.
"Well, actually it's only one word. Couldn't you replace[9] 'bread' with 'wine': The line should read: 'And give us our daily wine'"?
The Pope consulted[10] his secretaries; they checked all the old documents, then after a week the Pope called back.
"We are very interested in your suggestion[11], but I'm afraid, my son, we'll have to wait a little. Our contracts[12] with the Roman bakers don't expire[13] until the year 2222."

1 Schwierigkeiten 2 Produzent 3 daß seine Stunde gekommen sei 4 ein gutes Geschäft 5 Bilanz ausgleichen 6 ändern 7 Vaterunser 8 Welche Zeile meinst du? 9 ersetzen 10 sich beraten 11 Vorschlag 12 Verträge 13 auslaufen, erlöschen

Your Teletrainer

EXERCISE 1: Let's compare the two dialogues

Wie wird das Ende des Gesprächs angekündigt?	
Goodman – Dr. Brain	**Niemec – Slicer**
I'll h . . . to s . . . . now.	*When would it be a g . . . t . . . to c . . . you . . . .?*

Wie hält man den Kontakt weiterhin aufrecht?	
You'll g . . . me a r . . . when you get back, won't you?	*You can . . . e me there and I'll g . . . . . . to you immediately.*

Wie hat man sich verabschiedet?	
Well, ...	*B . . . . . now.*
T	*K . . . in . . . . . .*

EXERCISE 2: Let's be impatient

What do I h . . . to do to g . . you to . . . me . . . . – w . . . t . . . Christmas?

I can't k . . . w . . . . g. . . . . . . r

I've been h . . . . . . for . . . s

I haven't got . . . . . y

EXERCISE 3: Translation exercise

Wie wurde es gesagt?	
Mit wem spreche ich?	*Who* . . . . *to?*
Unsere Verbindung ist schlecht.	*We've* . . . .
Haben Sie meine Stimme nicht erkannt?	*Didn't* . . . .*?*
Rufen Sie mich an, wenn Sie zurück sind.	*You'll* . . . . *won't you?*
Dies ist ein Ferngespräch.	*This* . . . .
Sind Sie es, Niemec?	*Is* . . . . *?*
Bis bald.	*So* . . . .

Teletiquette: Where portables don't *come in handy*

come in handy – *praktisch sein*

Fred Niemec is sitting in a restaurant and while waiting for his steak, he takes our his *portable* and phones Tin Lizzy, Ltd. Fred might be one of those people who think they can *impress* others by drawing a cell phone in *public* and making and *receiving* calls. It's against telephone culture.

portable – *Handy*; *impress* – *beeindrucken*; *public* – *öffentlich*; *receiving* – *empfangen*

So *switch* your mobile phone *off*

switch off – *abschalten*

- in restaurants and in swimming pools
- during parties, at conferences and meetings
- and of course in the *presence* of friends or guests
- on board a plane or while *driving*.

presence – *Gegenwart*; *driving* – *Auto fahren*

If it is really *necessary* to use your phone, leave the room. Don't *bother* other people with your affairs.

necessary – *notwendig*; *bother* – *belästigen*

ROBOT RUNS RIOT

CONTENTS

Our Telestory:	Robot runs riot
Speech functions:	The language of complaint (2)
Teletiquette:	How to handle complaints on the telephone
Your Teletrainer:	Telephone culture
Teletactics:	What you should not say to a complainant
Your Teledoc:	Don't sell them a car – sell them feelings
Telejokes:	Time for a smile

Time for a smile

The secretary of a famous[1] Scottish psychiatrist[2] rang up Mr McNab: "Sir, I don't know how to put it. You may think I'm a nuisance, but the doctor is very disappointed[3] as you haven't paid the bill[4] we sent you three months ago. This problem has been giving him a headache[5]."
"Well", replied the Scotsman, "tell him to take two aspirins three times a day and if that doesn't help, call me back in two weeks."

1 berühmt 2 Psychiater 3 enttäuscht 4 Rechnung 5 Kopfweh

Robot *runs riot*

Amok laufen

Andrew Goodman goes *from strength to strength.* Robotalot delivered to Germany on time and Industry Services have already *put* the robot *to work.* Andrew *gets promotion* at Robotalot and becomes *area manager.* Perhaps he'll have more time for Fussy now.

von Erfolg zu Erfolg · *einsetzen* · *befördert werden* · *Gebietsleiter*

Fred's *fate* is different. He got a lot of problems with *delivery dates.* Tin Lizzy was late; he sold it much too cheap so his bosses were angry. *Eventually* Industry Services *put* the Tin Lizzy *into operation*, and then this.

Schicksal · *Liefertermine* · *schließlich* · *in Betrieb nehmen*

Fred Niemec (**F**), Herr Geiger (**G**)

F: Hello, Tin Lizzy, Ltd. Fred Niemec speaking. How can I help you?

G: Yes, that's a very good question. How can you help after all the *trouble* we've had?

Ärger

F: I'm sorry. I didn't catch your name. Mr eh ...?

G: Geiger, Industry Services. Purchasing director. I'm phoning to *express* my *anger* about that *scrap-iron* walking terminator which you sold us. I don't normally complain but ...

Ärger ausdrücken · *Schrott*

F: Now just a moment, sir. I don't quite follow you. Has Tin Lizzy I *misbehaved* in some way? These things are only *teething problems.*

sich danebenbenehmen · *Kinderkrankheiten*

G: Teething problems. Yes, we have problems with our *teeth*. Your Tin Lizzy was at a customer's. They switched on the function *'clean shelves'*. Instead of cleaning shelves at *head height* your *brain dead heap of plate metal* turned around and *smacked* the sales director in the mouth. He lost three teeth. Have you anything to say?

Zähne · *Regale säubern* · *Kopfhöhe* · *hirntoter Blechhaufen* · *schlagen*

F: Well, I'm sure things could have been *worse.*

schlimmer

G: They got much worse. Your *clinking* casanova robot seems to have a *weakness* for the

klappernd · *Schwäche*

opposite sex. We took him into the kitchen in a company. All he had to do was to *stretch* his arms out and grasp *piles of plates.* And what did he do but grab the *bottom* of one of the female employees ... It took three men twenty minutes to free the *unfortunate creature.*	*andere Geschlecht* · *ausstrecken* · *Stoß Teller* · *Hintern, Gesäß* · *unglückliche Geschöpf*
F: Ah, that's probably because Tin Lizzy has a *heat searching function.* He probably *locked onto* the warmest object in the area. Have you read the *handbook*?	*Hitzesensor · einrasten* · *Handbuch*
G: Look, I don't want to hear any excuses about your oversexed rambo-robot. I wish you goodday. You'll be hearing from our *lawyers.*	*Rechtsanwälte*

Speech functions: The language of complaint

(see also chapter 3)

I don't know how to put it.	Ich weiß nicht, wie ich es ausdrücken soll.
You may think I'm a nuisance, but I'm very disappointed.	Vielleicht halten Sie mich für aufdringlich, aber ich bin sehr enttäuscht.
I don't normally complain but in this case ...	Normalerweise beschwere ich mich nicht, aber in diesem Fall ...
I must register a serious complaint.	Ich habe eine schwerwiegende Reklamation.
I've a serious complaint to make.	Ich habe eine schwerwiegende Reklamation.
I'm phoning to express my anger about your robot.	Ich rufe an, um Ihnen zu sagen, wie verärgert ich über Ihren Roboter bin.
I don't want to hear any excuses.	Ich möchte keine Ausreden hören
You'll be hearing from our lawyers.	Sie hören von unseren Rechtsanwälten.

Time for a smile

A postman was complaining to his doctor that a dog had just bitten him in the leg.

Doctor: Did you put anything on it?
Postman: No, he liked it just as it was.

Teletiquette: How to handle complaints on the telephone

Customers who complain are like bombs that may explode. So *handle them with care* and *defuse* them. Here are the basic rules:	*behutsam behandeln* · *entschärfen*
1. Listen carefully and *take notes.*	*Notizen machen*
2. Don't *interrupt* the complainants.	*unterbrechen*
3. Ask *polite questions* until you have fully understood their problems.	*höfliche Fragen*
4. *Summarise* the complaint. That shows that you *take it seriously. Cooperate* with the customer.	*zusammenfassen* · *ernst nehmen · zusammenarbeiten*
5. *Apologise* but do not admit any fault or *deficiency* unless they are *proved.*	*sich entschuldigen* · *Fehler · bewiesen*
6. *Regard* a complaint as a chance to *improve* your product or services.	*betrachten · verbessern*
7. Never *put the blame on* another person or department in your company.	*die Schuld schieben auf*
8. Thank the customer for his criticism because he has helped you to *save money* in the future.	*Geld sparen*
9. *Complainants* should never be told to call back. It's your *duty* to return the call.	*Beschwerdeführer* · *Pflicht*
10. If the complaint *turns out* to be *unjustified,* give them the opportunity to save face. Allow them to *withdraw with their dignity intact.*	*sich herausstellen · ungerechtfertigt* · *sich zurückziehen ohne Gesichtsverlust*
11. If a complainant *becomes offensive,* you *suggest* that he should speak with your colleague or your boss.	*beleidigend werden · vorschlagen*
12. If you have to *terminate* the call, you could do it like this: I'm sorry – you are being offensive, and that won't *solve* the problem. I must ring off.	*beenden* · *lösen*

Your Teletrainer

EXERCISE 1: Telefunctions revised

Was sagt man nach dem Gruß?

- **Can I . . . . you?**
- **Can I be of a . . . . ?**
- **. . . . can I . . f . . you?**
- **At your . . . .**
- **Can I . . . . help?**
- **How can I help you?**

EXERCISE 2: What they really said

So war es gemeint:	So wurde es gesagt:
Fred Niemec here.	*Fred Niemec s . . . .*
What did you say your name was?	*I didn't c . . . . your . . . . .*
Could I just break in here?	*Now . . . . a m . . . . . , sir.*
Goodbye.	*I wish you g . . . .*

EXERCISE 3: Telephone culture

In the following dialogue people violate (verstoßen gegen) four of the twelve Basic Rules. If you think you have found them, tick them off (ankreuzen):

1	2	3	4	5	6	7	8	9	10	11	12

*(**S**) Switchboard, (**R**) Alf Rutland, a customer, (**D**) John Doorbar, advertisements*

S: *Late News. Good evening. Can I help you?*	
R: *I hope so. Put me through to the **advertising department**, will you? I've a **serious complaint** to make.*	*Annoncenabteilung* · *ernste Beschwerde*
S: *What did you say your name was?*	
R: *Rutland, Professor Rutland.*	
S: *Just a moment, sir. Putting you through.*	
D: *Advertising department. John Doorbar speaking. How can I be of help?*	
R: *I really want to complain most strongly about the way you've handled my adverts.*	
D: *What seems to be the **trouble**?*	*Problem*
R: *The trouble is that it wasn't there.*	
D: *Well ... hm ... Something must have happened.*	
R: *As far as I can see nothing has happened at all. **Moreover,** when I **finally** saw the ad last Friday it was full of mistakes.*	*darüber hinaus · endlich*
D: *Oh, dear. What sort of mistakes?*	
R: *The advert was for a 'mad wife'. I can't **accept** ...*	*hinnehmen, akzeptieren*
D: *Now, just a moment, sir. A **mad** wife? I'm afraid I don't understand.*	*verrückt*
R: *At first, we didn't either. After having interviewed the first dozen **applicants**, we checked the advert. **It should have read 'midwife'.***	*Bewerber* · *Es hätte lauten sollen · Hebamme*
D: *Maybe our secretary got it wrong because you speak very fast. She's Irish, you know. **Misunder-***	*Mißverständnis*

standings *like that can happen on the telephone. Next time you had better do it in writing. Any other details?*	
R: *Well, another little detail is the* ***payment*** *for the advert. Tell your boss you will not be* ***receiving*** *it. Wait a minute, I'll tell him myself. Goodbye.*	*Bezahlung* *erhalten*

Teletactics

What you should not say to a dissatisfied customer	
Things like that can happen in any business.	So etwas kann in jeder Firma passieren.
Have you read the handbook?	Haben Sie das Handbuch gelesen?
These things are only teething problems.	Dies sind nur Kinderkrankheiten.
I'm afraid you're out of warranty.	Leider ist Ihre Garantie abgelaufen.
I can't agree with you.	Ich bin da anderer Meinung.
Can you prove that it's our fault?	Können Sie beweisen, daß wir schuld sind?
We've have been selling this article for years and we've never had any complaints.	Wir verkaufen den Artikel seit Jahren und haben noch nie Klagen gehabt.
You are the first to complain about our robot.	Sie sind der erste, der unseren Roboter reklamiert.
We haven't had any complaints so far.	Wir haben bisher noch keine Beschwerden gehabt.

Your Teledoc: Don't sell them a car – sell them feelings

Human beings are complex. Visual, auditive or emotional types do not exist as pure, ideal types. Most people are combinations of two or all three. So you if you want to *be on the safe side, appeal to all senses* – to the eye of the visual type, to the ear of the auditive type and to the *emotions* of the kinesthetic type. Let's take an example. How would you – as a clever car salesman – *go about it*?

sicher gehen
Sinne ansprechen
Gefühle
anstellen

Since you can't show a car on the phone you have to use words. Don't sell them an abstract car – sell them *colourful* images, *pleasant* sounds and feelings.

da
farbig · angenehm

Make them hear the *humming* of a powerful *engine*, make them feel its vibration at their *fingertips* when they touch the mahogany *steering wheel*, the softness of the seats. And how it *absorbs* all the shocks of a *bumpy* road! Talk about the perfume of *smooth* leather, about the car's elegant, aerodynamic form and its sexy *curves*.

Summen
Motor
Fingerspitzen
Steuerrad
schlucken · holprig
glatt, weich
Kurven

By the way, this is what *advertising* and selling is all about. Presenting yourself and your product isn't much different from advertising. On the phone you can *create* a reality of your own. Your listener is not able to *compare* your words with the reality. You can do things on the phone which are impossible in a *face to face* situation. An *insignificant* small, fat salesman can sound like Kevin Kostner. That is why the phone is such a powerful *tool* in the hands of those who know how to *handle* it.

Werbung
erschaffen
vergleichen
von Angesicht zu Angesicht
unscheinbar
Instrument
umgehen

Chapter 22

EPILOGUE: TURNING OVER A NEW PAGE[1]

CONTENTS

Our Telestory:	**Permanent holiday for Fred Niemec**
Telefunctions:	**Messages and announcements on answering machines**
Our Telejoke:	**Time for a smile**

Time for a smile

Bell invented[2] the telephone, but he found it was useless[3] until[4] he invented the second telephone.
This was fine, until he invented the third telephone, phoned the second, and found it engaged[5].

1 ein neues Leben anfangen 2 erfinden 3 nutzlos 4 bis 5 besetzt

Permanent holiday	*Dauerurlaub*
To cut a long story short Fred Niemec's days as a salesman were *numbered*. Of course it wasn't his *fault*. Life is sometimes very unfair. A week or so later Fred arrived at his flat. He listened to his new *automatic answering* machine. He was very *proud* of the new message he had *recorded* on it. "Hello, here is your super salesperson. *If it moves, sell it*. That's my motto. So if you want to contact me leave your message starting now."	*gezählt* *Schuld* *Anrufbeantworter* *stolz · aufnehmen* *Was nicht niet- und nagelfest ist, wird verkauft*
On this day there was a message on the machine. Fred had a bad feeling as he began to listen:	
"Hello Niemec, this is Slicer, Marketing Director from Tin Lizzy. Look, I'll come *straight to the point*. The managing director was highly *dissatisfied* with your *performance* in Germany. It cost the company a lot of money. So basically you're invited to take a holiday ... *permanently*! Good luck with your future projects. Goodbye."	*direkt zur Sache* *unzufrieden* *Leistung* *für immer*
Fred Niemec (**N**) is not depressed. He phones his local job centre (**R**):	
R: Broadward Job Centre. Can I help you?	
N: Hello. My name's Niemec. Could you put me through to the director of '*executive positions*', please?	*Führungspositionen*
R: Yes. Could you repeat your name, please?	
N: N i e m e c.	
R: Sorry sir, could you spell that, please?	
N: Nellie-Isaac-Edward-Mary-Edward-Charlie. *Got it?*	*Haben Sie's*
R: Thank you. I'm afraid my boss isn't in. Can I take a message?	
N: Yes, I'd like to make an *appointment* with him to discuss my future.	*Termin*
R: I see. Well, could you ring back tomorrow? He might be in then.	
N: Well, thank-you very much. Goodbye.	

Telefunctions: Answering machines and announcements

This is a recorded message.	Dies ist eine Bandaufnahme.
Our telephone number has been changed.	Unsere Rufnummer hat sich geändert.
You can phone us on 33 44 54.	Sie erreichen uns unter 33 44 54.
This is the automatic answering machine of Tin Lizzy, Ltd.	Hier ist der automatische Anrufbeantworter der Firma Tin Lizzy, Ltd.
This phone is not in use at the moment.	Dieser Apparat ist im Augenblick nicht besetzt.
Sorry, we cannot be reached at the moment.	Wir sind im Augenblick leider nicht erreichbar.
You have telephoned outside office hours.	Sie rufen außerhalb unserer Bürozeiten an.
Please, leave a message.	Hinterlassen Sie uns bitte eine Nachricht.
We'll ring you back as soon as possible.	Wir rufen Sie baldmöglichst zurück.
Please speak after the tone.	Sprechen Sie bitte nach dem Signalton.
Please leave your message after the tone.	Hinterlassen Sie bitte eine Nachricht nach dem Signalton.
Sorry, we are out. But leave your name, number and message and we'll be in touch.	Wir sind leider nicht erreichbar. Hinterlassen Sie Ihren Namen, Telefonnummer und eine Nachricht. Wir rufen Sie zurück.
You are calling PELC Seminar. Our office is open from Monday to Friday from 9 a.m. to 4 p.m.	Sie sind mit PELC Seminar verbunden. Unser Büro ist geöffnet von Montag bis Freitag zwischen 9 Uhr und 16 Uhr.
Thank-you for calling.	Danke für Ihren Anruf.

Tin Lizzy in Tokio: Smiling robot is face of the future

A robot that can show emotion with a *grin* or	*Lächeln, Grinsen*
a *grimace* may help people to deal as easily with	*Grimasse*
machines as they do with each other, according to a Japanese professor.	
Not satisfied with robots that work carefully	
and *efficiently* Prof. Fumio Hara of the Science	*leistungsfähig*
University of Tokyo wants them to do it with a smile, writes the "Daily Telegraph."	
He believes that expressions may account for as much as 55 per cent of communication between people.	
After more than a decade working on the concept, including a year studying how more than 40 seperate movements can create all human	
facial expressions Prof. Hara has unveiled his	*Gesichtsausdruck*
£ 62,500 Face Robot.	
Three years in development, a computer uses the robot to express six emotions to its human	
masters – *anger*, sadness, fear, surprise, happi-	*Zorn, Ärger*
ness and *disgust*. Its skin is made of silicon	*Empörung, Abscheu*
rubber and its 24 muscles are *hydraulic pistons.*	*hydraulische Kolben*
The Face Robot sees through video cameras placed behind its eyeballs. These feed an	
image to an *artificial* intelligence program that	*künstlich*
the research team is developing to analyse	
human expression, so the robot can *adopt* the	*übernehmen*
right expression *in response.*	*als Reaktion*
This would make the machines more people-friendly. Prof. Hara believes the Face Robot could be used in hospitals and even help doctors and entertainers to express themselves.	

Entnommen aus World and Press

THE COMPLETE THEMATIC LIST OF TELEFUNCTIONS

Die englische Sprache ist reich an Ausdrücken gleicher Bedeutung. Deshalb finden Sie für einen deutschen Satz oft mehrere englische Sätze mit ähnlicher Bedeutung. Deshalb kann man nicht für alle englischen Redemittel eine idiomatische deutsche Entsprechung finden.

1. Anrufe entgegennehmen: Wie Sie sich als Firma melden

Robotalot. Guten Morgen.	*Robotalot. Good morning.*
Satco. Sie wünschen?	*Satco. Can I help you?*
Guten Tag. Kann ich Ihnen helfen?	*Good morning. Can I help you?*
Satco. Guten Tag. Kann ich Ihnen helfen?	*Satco. Hello. Can I be of help?*
Guten Tag. Was kann ich für Sie tun?	*Hello. How can I help you?*
Kann ich Ihnen helfen?	*May I help you?*
Womit kann ich dienen?	*How can I be of assistance?*
Was kann ich für Sie tun?	*What can I do for you?*
Satco Limited. Womit können wir dienen?	*Satco Limited at your service.*
Kann ich sonst noch etwas für Sie tun?	*Anything else I can do for you?*
Was kann ich noch für Sie tun?	*Can I assist you in any other way?*

2. Anrufe machen : Sagen Sie, wer Sie sind

Hier ist Jack Brown. Guten Morgen.	*Jack Brown here. Good morning.*
Hier spricht Tom Smith von der Firma Satco.	*This is Tom Smith of Satco speaking.*
Hier ist Susan Child, Dr. Brains Sekretärin.	*This is Susan Child, Dr. Brain's secretary.*
Ich gebe Ihnen meinen Namen. Ich heiße Brain, Brian Brain.	*I'll give you my name. It's Brain, Brian Brain.*
Ich gebe Ihnen Name und Adresse.	*I'll just let you have my name and address.*
Meine Privatnummer ist 83 33 24.	*My home number is 83 33 24.*
Meine Privatnummer ist 83 33 24.	*My private number is 83 33 24.*
Im Büro erreichen Sie mich unter 78 79 96.	*In the office you can reach me on 78 79 96.*
Während der Arbeitszeit erreichen Sie mich unter 33 04 04.	*My number at work is 33 04 04.*

the dialling code for Berlin is 03

Die Nummer meiner Firma ist 33 04 04.	*My company number is double three o four o four.*
Ich habe Apparat Nummer ...	*My extension is ...*
Die Vorwahlnummer ist ...	*The area code is ...*
Die Vorwahlnummer von London ist 01.	*The dialling code for London is 01.*
Die Vorwahlnummer von Deutschland ist 00 49.	*The country code for Germany is 00 49.*

3. Nennen Sie den Grund Ihres Anrufs

Es geht um Ihr Angebot.	*It's about your quotation.*
Ich rufe wegen des Zeitungsinserats an.	*I'm ringing about your advert.*
Es handelt sich um Ihre Anzeige.	*It's in connection with your advert.*
Ich rufe im Zusammenhang mit ... an.	*I'm calling in connection with ...*
Ich rufe an, um mich über die freie Stelle zu erkundigen.	*I'm calling to ask about the vacancy.*
Ich rufe wegen der freien Stelle an.	*I'm phoning concerning the vacancy.*
Ich hätte gerne ein paar Informationen über ...	*I'd like some information about ...*
Ich rufe an, um Informationen über Ihre Roboter einzuholen.	*I'm calling to get some information about your robots.*
Ich rufe wegen einer Reklamation an.	*I'm calling to make a complaint.*
Ich rufe für Dr. Brain an.	*I'm ringing up for Dr. Brain.*
Ich rufe im Auftrag von Dr. Brain an.	*I'm calling on behalf of Dr. Brain ...*
Ich rufe an, um Ihre Reservierung zu bestätigen.	*I'm phoning to confirm your reservation.*
Ich rufe an, um Ihnen die Einzelheiten über ... mitzuteilen.	*I'm ringing to let you know the details of ...*
Ich rufe an, um Ihnen einige Einzelheiten über unser Angebot mitzuteilen.	*I'm phoning to give you some details about our quotation.*
Ich rufe an, um Ihnen über ... zu erzählen.	*I'm calling to tell you about ...*
Der Grund meines Anrufs ist ...	*The reason why I'm calling is ...*
Lassen Sie mich gleich zur Sache kommen.	*Let me come straight to the point.*
Ich würde Dr. Brain gerne geschäftlich sprechen.	*I'd like to speak to Dr. Brain on business.*
Ich möchte Dr. Brain in einer Privatangelegenheit sprechen.	*I'd like to speak to Dr. Brain about a private matter.*
Ich glaube, es ist besser, ich spreche mit ihm persönlich.	*I think I'd better speak to him personally.*
Ich habe eine Bitte.	*I've a request to make.*

4. So identifizieren Sie den Anrufer

Dr. Brain. Sind Sie es, Goodman?	*Dr. Brain speaking, is that you Goodman?*
Wer ist bitte am Apparat?	*Who is calling, please?*
Bin ich mit Robotalot in München verbunden?	*Is that Robotalot in Munich?*
Spreche ich mit Robotalot in Bonn?	*Am I speaking to Robotalot in Bonn?*
Wer ist am Apparat?	*Who is (that) speaking?*
Wer ist bitte am Apparat?	*Who is on the line, please?*
Wie heißen Sie bitte?	*What's your name please?*
Kann ich bitte Ihren Namen haben?	*Could I have your name, please?*
Darf ich um Ihren Namen bitten?	*May I ask who is calling?*
Mit wem spreche ich bitte?	*Could I ask who I'm speaking to?*
Würden Sie mir bitte Ihren Namen nennen?	*Could you give me your name, please?*
Darf ich Ihren Namen erfahren?	*Could I ask your name, please?*
Verzeihung, wie war Ihr Name?	*Pardon, what did you say your name was?*
Entschuldigen Sie, aber ich habe Ihren Namen nicht richtig verstanden.	*I'm sorry, sir. I didn't quite catch your name.*
Entschuldigen Sie, wie, sagten Sie, war Ihr Name?	*I beg your pardon, what did you say your name was?*
Wen darf ich bitte melden?	*Who shall I say is calling?*
Können Sie das bitte buchstabieren?	*Could you spell that, please?*
Von wo rufen Sie an?	*Where are you calling from?*
Schreiben Sie Brian mit 'i' oder 'y'?	*Do you spell Brian with an 'i' or a 'y'?*
Schreibt sich Tickersun mit 'D' oder mit 'T'?	*Tickersun, is that with a 'D' or a 'T'?*
Von welcher Firma sind Sie?	*What company are you from?*
Herr Brain ... von welcher Firma, bitte?	*Mr Brain ... from which company, please?*
Können Sie mir bitte sagen, von wo Sie anrufen?	*Can you tell me where you are ringing from, please?*
Könnten Sie bitte den Namen Ihrer Firma buchstabieren?	*Could you please spell the name of your company?*
Und wie ist bitte Ihre Adresse?	*And what's the address, please?*
Und wie ist bitte Ihre Adresse?	*And what address is that, please?*
Entschuldigen Sie, wie, sagten Sie, war Ihre Adresse?	*Sorry, what did you say your address was?*
Könnten Sie mir bitte auch die Postleitzahl geben?	*Could you give me the post code as well, please?*
Möchten Sie Ihren Namen und Ihre Adresse hinterlassen?	*Would you like to leave me your name and address?*

Wären Sie so freundlich, mir auch Ihre Privatnummer zu geben?	*Would you be kind enough to give me your home number, too?*
Wer hat da eben angerufen?	*Who was that on the phone?*
Wer war da eben am Apparat?	*Who was that on the phone just now?*
Ich weiß nicht? Er hat aufgelegt.	*I don't know. He's put the receiver down.*
Keine Ahnung. Er hat eingehängt.	*No idea. He's hung up.*
Weiß ich nicht. Falsch verbunden.	*I don't know. Wrong number.*
Bist du's, Andrew?	*Is that you, Andrew?*
Hast du meine Stimme nicht erkannt.	*Didn't you recognize my voice?*

5. Fragen Sie nach dem Grund des Anrufs

Würden Sie mir bitte den Grund Ihres Anrufs nennen?	*Would you mind telling me what you are calling about?*
Darf ich nach dem Grund Ihres Anrufs fragen?	*Could I ask the purpose of you call?*
Könnten Sie mir kurz sagen, warum Sie anrufen?	*Could you give me some idea why you are calling?*
Würden Sie mir bitte sagen, was der Grund Ihres Anrufs ist?	*Would it be possible for you to give some idea about the reason for your call?*
Was ist der Grund Ihres Anrufs?	*Well, what's the reason for your call?*
Darf ich fragen, um was es geht?	*May I ask what it's all about?*
Um was geht es, bitte?	*What's it in connection with?*
Und was betrifft es, bitte?	*And what does it concern, please?*
Darf ich fragen, worum es geht?	*Could I ask what it is concerned with?*
Wen wünschen Sie zu sprechen?	*Who would you like to speak to?*
In welcher Abteilung arbeitet er / sie?	*Which department is he / she in?*
Kennt Frau Child den Grund Ihres Anrufs?	*Will Mrs Child know what you are calling about?*
Es ist vertraulich.	*It's confidential.*
Es ist etwas Privates.	*It's a private matter.*

6. Sagen Sie, wen Sie zu sprechen wünschen

Geben Sie mir bitte Ihre Verkaufsabteilung.	*Could you put me through to your sales department, please?*
Geben Sie mir bitte Apparat 344.	*Could I have extension 344, please?*
Ich hätte gerne Apparat 222.	*I'd like extension 222.*
Guten Tag. Herrn Bill Smith bitte.	*Hello, Mr Bill Smith, please.*
Seien Sie so freundlich, und verbinden Sie mich mit Bill Smith.	*Hello, could you put me through to Bill Smith, please?*
Wären Sie so freundlich, mich mit Herrn Brain zu verbinden?	*Would you be so kind as to put me through to Mr Brain?*

Grüß Gott. Ist Herr Jones da? Ich würde gerne mit ihm sprechen.	*Hello, is Mr Jones in? I'd like to speak to him.*
Ich würde gerne Herrn Brain sprechen, wenn das möglich ist.	*I'd like to speak to Mr Brain, if it's possible.*
Ich würde gerne Herrn Brain sprechen, wenn es geht.	*I'd like to speak to Mr Brain, if I may.*
Könnte ich Herrn Tickersun sprechen, wenn das möglich ist?	*Could I speak to Mr Tickersun, please, if that is possible.*
Wäre es möglich, mit Frau Child zu sprechen, falls sie da ist?	*Could I possibly speak to Mrs Child, if she's in?*
Ist es möglich, Herrn Jones zu sprechen?	*Would it be possible to speak to Mr Jones?*
Könnte ich ihn kurz sprechen?	*Could I just have a word with him?*
Könnte ich Herrn Brain kurz sprechen?	*Could I have a quick word with Mr Brain?*
Ich müßte Herrn Brain kurz sprechen.	*I need a quick word with Mr Brain.*
Verbinden Sie mich bitte mit Tim Jones.	*Put me through to Tim Jones, please.*
Ob Sie mich wohl mit Herrn Smith verbinden könnten?	*I wonder if you could put me through to Mr Smith?*
Ist Herr Brain über das Autotelefon erreichbar?	*Can Mr Brain be reached by car phone?*
Hat Herr Brain einen Piepser bei sich?	*Has Mr Brain got a pager?*
Könnten Sie bitte versuchen, ihn anzupiepsen?	*Could you please try to get him on the pager?*
Könnten Sie ihn bitte anpiepsen/ausrufen?	*Could you please page him?*
	Could you try paging him?
Verbinden Sie mich bitte mit Herrn ...	*Please put me through to Mr ...*
Sein Name ist mir entfallen.	*his name has slipped my mind.*
Ich erinnere mich nicht mehr so recht an seinen Namen.	*I can't quite remember his name.*
Sie wissen nicht zufällig ihren Vornamen?	*You wouldn't happen to know her first name?*
Sie wissen nicht zufällig seinen Namen?	*You don't know his name, by any chance?*
Ich muß dringend mit dem Direktor sprechen, wenn es geht.	*I really need to speak to the director, if I might.*
Es ist sehr wichtig, daß ich mit ihm spreche.	*It's very important that I get into contact with him.*
Geben Sie mir bitte Herrn Slicer.	*Please put me through to Mr Slicer.*
Es ist ein Notfall.	*It's an emergency.*

7. Private Anrufe

Hier ist Tom.	*It's me, Tom*
Ich bin's, Tom.	*Tom here.*
Hallo. Ich bin's, Tom.	*Hi, this is Tom.*
Tickersun am Apparat.	*Tickersun speaking.*
Tom Bradley am Apparat.	*It's Tom Bradley speaking.*
Dieses Gespräch ist vertraulich. Kannst du frei sprechen, oder bist du nicht allein?	*This is a private call. Can you speak freely or is someone else in the room?*
Hallo, wer ist am Apparat?	*Hi, who's there?*
Wer ist da?	*Who is that?*
Ich bin's, Anne.	*It's Anne here.*
Ich hätte gerne Tom gesprochen, falls er aus dem Urlaub zurück ist.	*I'd like to speak to Tom, if he's back from his holiday.*
Ich hätte gerne Ihren Mann gesprochen, wenn es geht.	*I'd like to speak to your husband, if I may.*
Ich würde gerne Tom sprechen.	*I'd like to speak to Tom.*
Am Apparat.	*Speaking.*
Ist Fred da?	*Is Fred in?*
Ich sehe nach, ob er da ist.	*I'll just see if he's in.*
Ja, Tom ist da. Ich hole ihn an den Apparat.	*Yes, Tom is in. I'll put him on for you.*
Tom, da ist ein Gespräch für dich.	*Tom, a call for you.*
Ich habe schon ewig nichts mehr von dir gehört!	*I haven't heard from you for ages!*

8. Worte des Verbindens

Können Sie mich bitte verbinden?	*Can you transfer me, please?*
Verbinden Sie mich bitte mit Fred Niemec.	*Please connect me with Fred Niemec.*
Könnten Sie mich mit Herrn X verbinden?	*Could you put me through to Mr X?*
Ich stelle Sie durch.	*I'm putting you through.*
Bleiben Sie bitte am Apparat!	*Hold on, please.*
Bleiben Sie bitte dran!	*Hold the line, please.*
Bleiben Sie am Apparat! Sie werden verbunden.	*Hold the line. You are connected now.*
Sind Sie noch am Apparat?	*Are you still holding?*
Augenblick. Ich stelle Sie durch.	*Just a moment please. Putting you through.*
Ich versuche eben Sie zu verbinden. Bleiben Sie bitte am Apparat.	*Trying to connect you. Hold the line, please.*
Einen Augenblick. Ich versuche das Gespräch auf ihren Apparat zu legen.	*One moment, I'll try her desk.*

Ich verbinde Sie mit ihrem Sekretär.	*I'm connecting you with her secretary.*
Ich verbinde Sie mit der richtigen Abteilung.	*I'm transferring you to the right department.*
Ich gebe Ihnen den Sachbearbeiter.	*I'll transfer you to the person responsible.*
Sie müssen vermutlich mit Herrn Brodie sprechen.	*You'll need to speak to Mr Brodie.*
Ich glaube, da müssen Sie mit ihrer Sekretärin sprechen.	*I guess you should speak to her secretary.*
Einen Augenblick. Sie werden verbunden.	*Just one moment. It's ringing for you.*
Dr. Brains Telefon läutet bereits.	*Dr. Brain's number is ringing.*
Sie können sprechen./ Sie sind verbunden.	*You're through now.*
Herr Brain kann Ihren Anruf entgegennehmen. Sprechen Sie bitte.	*Go ahead, Mr Brain can take your call.*
Herr Brown, Sie werden am Telefon gewünscht. Es ist Herr Black.	*Mr Brown, you are wanted on the phone. It's Mr Black.*
Ich verbinde Sie mit der Kundendienst-abteilung.	*I'll pass you over to Customer Service.*
Tut mir leid, ich kann ihn nicht erreichen.	*Sorry, I can't get his number.*
Ich gebe das Gespräch zurück an die Vermittlung.	*I'll pass / hand you (back) to the switchboard.*

9. Trost für Wartende

Tut mir leid, wenn ich Sie warten ließ.	*Sorry to keep you waiting.*
Tut mir leid, daß ich Sie habe warten lassen.	*Sorry to have kept you waiting.*
Tut mir leid, aber ich erreiche die Nummer nicht.	*Sorry, but I can't get this number.*
Bedaure, ich kann diese Nummer nicht erreichen.	*Sorry, I can't reach this number.*
Frau Potter spricht gerade auf einer anderen Leitung.	*Mrs Potter is speaking on another line.*
Es tut mir leid, aber ihre Leitung ist immer noch besetzt.	*I am sorry but her line is still engaged.*
Sie ist jetzt frei.	*She is available now.*
Ich versuche immer noch Sie zu verbinden.	*I'm still trying to connect you.*
Die Leitung ist leider belegt.	*I'm afraid the line is engaged.*
Tut mir sehr leid, aber es wird gerade gesprochen.	*I'm awfully sorry, but the line is busy.*
Die Nebenstelle/ der Apparat meldet sich nicht.	*There's no reply from the extension.*
Ich gebe Sie zurück an die Zentrale.	*I'll pass / hand you back to the switchboard.*

Legen Sie nicht auf. Ich verbinde.	*Don't hang up. I'll put you through.*
Können Sie dranbleiben?	*Can you hold?*
Möchten Sie warten?	*Do you want to hold?*
Möchten Sie warten?	*Will you hold?*
Bleiben Sie am Apparat.	*Hold the line!*
Bleiben Sie bitte dran.	*Hold on, please!*
Wenn Sie einen Moment dranbleiben, versuche ich es noch einmal.	*If you hold a moment, I'll try again.*
Bleiben Sie bitte am Apparat.	*Please hold the line.*
Möchten Sie warten?	*Would you like to hold?*
Ich melde mich gleich wieder.	*I'll be with you in a minute.*
Ich melde mich gleich wieder	*I'll be back to you in a minute.*

10. Ungeduld und Verärgerung spüren lassen

Dies ist ein Ferngespräch. Ich kann nicht länger warten.	*This is a long-distance call. I can't hold any longer.*
Ich kann nicht ewig warten.	*I can't keep waiting for ever.*
Vermittlung, ich warte nun schon eine Ewigkeit.	*Operator, I've been holding for ages.*
Das war eine verdammt lange Minute.	*That was a damn long minute.*
Würden Sie mich verbinden, wenn Ihnen das nicht zu viele Umstände macht?	*Would you put me through, if it's not too much trouble?*
Was muß ich noch tun, damit Sie mich verbinden, etwa bis Weihnachten warten?	*What do I have to do to get you to put me through, wait until Chistmas?*
Ich werde jedesmal unterbrochen, wenn ich Herrn Brains Nummer wähle.	*I get cut off every time I dial Mr Brain's number.*
Dies ist nun schon das zweite Mal, daß Sie mich mit der falschen Abteilung verbinden.	*This is the second time you have put me through to the wrong department.*
Sie haben mir schon wieder den falschen Apparat gegeben.	*You've given me the wrong extension again.*
Ich möchte Ihren Chef persönlich sprechen.	*I want to speak to your boss personally.*
Es ist in seinem, nicht in meinem Interesse.	*It's in his interest, not mine.*
Herr Tickersun wird sehr ärgerlich sein, wenn Sie mich nicht sofort mit ihm verbinden.	*Mr Tickersun will be very angry if you don't put me through to him immediately.*
Ich weiß, daß Herr Tickersun da ist. Ich habe vor fünf Minuten mit ihm telefoniert.	*I know that Mr Tickersun is in. I was on the phone to him five minutes ago.*
Ich rate Ihnen, mich jetzt zu verbinden, oder ich storniere den Auftrag für Ihre Firma.	*I advise you to put me through now or I'll cancel the order with your company.*

Haben Sie Geduld. Es dauert nicht lange.	*Please be patient. It won't take long.*
Bitte beruhigen Sie sich. Ich tue mein Bestes.	*Please calm down. I'm doing my best*
Ihr Bestes genügt aber nicht.	*Your best isn't good enough.*
Würden Sie mir bitte Ihren Namen sagen?	*Could you give me your name, please?*
Ich werde mich über Sie beschweren.	*I'm going to complain about you.*
Gehen Sie aus meiner Leitung.	*Stop listening on the line.*
Gehen Sie aus der Leitung! Dies ist ein privates Gespräch.	*Get off the line! This is a private call.*

11. So unterbrechen Sie den Redefluß

Langsam, langsam! / Einen Augenblick!	*Now just a moment!*
Entschuldigen Sie, aber ...	*Excuse me but ...*
Könnte ich dazu kurz was sagen?	*Could I just break in here?*
Entschuldigen Sie, aber ich muß Sie leider unterbrechen.	*Sorry, but I really must interrupt you.*

12. Entschuldigungen am Telefon

Entschuldigen Sie bitte, daß ich Sie nicht zurückgerufen habe.	*Excuse me for not having called you back.*
Entschuldigen Sie bitte, daß ich in Ihrer Mittagspause anrufe.	*Excuse me for calling during your lunch break.*
Tut mir leid, ich dachte, es wäre ein Vertreter.	*I'm so sorry, I thought it was a salesman.*
Entschuldigen Sie bitte, ich muß mich wohl verwählt haben.	*I beg your pardon, I must have dialled the wrong number.*

13. Ein Gespräch übergeben und übernehmen

Nehmen Sie das Gespräch an?	*Are you going to take the call?*
Natürlich nehme ich das Gespräch an.	*Of course. I'll take it.*
Da ist ein Herr Smith für Sie am Apparat. Soll ich das Gespräch auf Ihren Apparat legen?	*There's a Mr Smith for you on the phone. Shall I transfer him to your extension?*
Ist es Ihnen recht, wenn ich das Gespräch auf Ihren Apparat lege?	*Is it okay if I put the call through to your extension?*
Würden Sie bitte ans Telefon gehen?	*Would you please answer the phone?*
Würden Sie bitte den Hörer abnehmen?	*Would you please lift the receiver?*
Apparat von Herrn Dr. Brain. Sie sprechen mit Frau Child.	*Dr. Brain's phone, Mrs Child speaking.*

14. Wenn Gesprächspartner nicht erreichbar sind

Frau Child ist nicht an ihrem Platz.	*Mrs Child is not at her desk.*
Tut mir leid. Dr. Brain ist im Augenblick nicht im Büro.	*I'm sorry, Dr. Brain is out of the office at the moment.*
Er ist im Augenblick nicht hier.	*He isn't here at the moment.*
Er ist noch nicht da.	*He isn't in yet.*
Ich glaube, Frau Child ist wohl in der Mittagspause.	*I think Mrs Child might be on her lunch break.*
Und Herr Smith ist zum Mittagessen.	*And Mr Smith is out for lunch.*
Tut mir leid, er ist nicht da. Kann ich etwas ausrichten?	*Sorry, he isn't in. Can I take a message?*
Tut mir leid, aber die Leitung ist besetzt.	*Sorry, but the line is engaged.*
Möchten Sie am Apparat bleiben?	*Do you want to hold?*
Er spricht gerade auf der anderen Leitung.	*He's on another line at the moment.*
Sie sind leider unterbrochen worden. Ich versuche es noch einmal.	*I'm afraid you've been cut off. I'll try again.*
Es nimmt niemand ab. Versuchen Sie es später noch einmal.	*There's no reply. Try again later.*
Der Teilnehmer meldet sich nicht. Soll ich etwas ausrichten?	*There's no answer. Shall I take a message?*
Herr Brain ist im Augenblick leider nicht erreichbar.	*I'm afraid Mr Brain is not available at the moment.*
Tut mir leid, aber Herr Brain hat diese Woche Urlaub.	*I'm sorry, but Mr Brain is on holiday this week.*
Ich fürchte, sie kommt diese Woche nicht ins Büro.	*I'm afraid she is out of the office this week.*
Ich sehe nach, wo er ist.	*I' ll check where he is.*
Ich höre, daß er heute außer Hause ist.	*I've just been told he's out today.*
Herr Brain ist geschäftlich unterwegs.	*Mr Brain is away on business.*
Bedaure, Herr Brain ist in einer Besprechung.	*I'm sorry Mr Brain is at a meeting.*
Tut mir leid, Herr Brain ist augenblicklich nicht im Büro.	*I'm afraid, he's out of the office at the moment.*
Er ist mitten in einem Vorstellungsgespräch.	*He's in the middle of an interview for a job.*
Er hat gerade einen wichtigen Besucher.	*He has got an important visitor just now.*
Dr. Brain wird in Kürze zurück sein.	*Dr. Brain is expected back shortly.*
Kann ich Ihnen irgendwie helfen?	*Is there anything I can do for you?*
Könnte Ihnen vielleicht ihre Sekretärin weiterhelfen?	*Could her secretary help you?*

Möchten Sie mit jemand anderem sprechen?	*Would you like to speak to someone else?*
Um wieviel Uhr erwarten Sie Dr. Brain zurück?	*At what time is Dr. Brain expected back?*
Können Sie mir sagen, wann ich ihn am ehesten antreffe?	*Can you tell me when I am most likely to find him in?*
Können Sie mir bitte die Vermittlung noch mal geben?	*Can you let me have the operator again, please?*

15. Eine Nachricht hinterlassen

Würden Sie ihm bitte ausrichten, daß Bob Marley angerufen hat?	*Would you please tell him that Bob Marley called?*
Wären Sie so freundlich, ihm etwas auszurichten?	*Would you be so kind as to pass a message on to him?*
Könnten Sie ihm sagen, daß ich angerufen habe?	*Could you please tell him I phoned?*
Könnte ich eine Nachricht hinterlassen?	*Could I leave a message, please?*
Wäre es möglich, eine Nachricht zu hinterlassen?	*Would it be possible to leave a message?*
Könnten Sie ihm etwas ausrichten?	*Could you give him a message?*
Würden Sie John etwas von mir ausrichten?	*Would you give John a message for me?*
Kann ich ihm ein paar Zeilen hinterlassen?	*Can I leave a note for him?*
Könnten Sie ihm eine Nachricht von mir ausrichten?	*Could you pass on a message for me?*
Könnten Sie ihn bitte fragen, ob ...?	*Would you please ask him, if ...?*
Könnten Sie Dr. Brain bitten, mich zurückzurufen?	*Could you ask Dr. Brain to call me back?*
Teilen Sie ihm bitte mit, daß ich heute keine Zeit habe.	*Could you let him know that I won't be free today?*
Haben Sie es?	*Have you got it? / Got it?*

16. Nachrichten entgegennehmen

Kann ich etwas ausrichten?	*Can I take a message?*
Kann ich Herrn Brain etwas ausrichten?	*Can I pass on a message to Mr Brain?*
Kann ich ihm etwas ausrichten?	*Could I take a message for him?*
Möchten Sie ihm eine Nachricht hinterlassen?	*Would you like to leave a message for him?*
Soll ich das aufschreiben?	*Shall I note that down?*

Ich werde dafür sorgen, daß er Ihre Nachricht erhält.	*I'll make sure that he gets your message.*
Ich kümmere mich darum, daß Frau Child Ihre Nachricht erhält.	*I'll see that Mrs Child get's your message.*
Ich gebe das an Frau Child weiter.	*I'll pass that on to Mrs Child.*
Soll ich ihn bitten, Sie zurückzurufen?	*Shall I ask him to call you back?*
Hat Frau Child Ihre Nummer?	*Does Mrs Child have your number?*
Hat Frau Child Ihre Nummer?	*Has Mrs Child got your number?*
Und wie ist Ihre Rufnummer bitte?	*And what's your phone number, please?*
Haben Sie eine Nummer, unter der wir Sie erreichen können?	*Do you have a telephone number we can contact you on?*
Und wann wäre es für Sie günstig, daß Tom Sie anruft?	*When would it be a good time for Tom to call you back?*
Wann würde es Ihnen passen?	*When would it be convenient for you?*
Wann würde es Ihnen passen?	*When would it suit you?*
Würde Ihnen Dienstag um neun Uhr passen?	*Would Tuesday, nine o'clock be a convenient time?*
Sie hören von Herrn Brain am späteren Vormittag.	*You will be hearing from Mr Brain later in the morning.*
Hat jemand für mich angerufen?	*Have there been any calls for me?*
Hat jemand für mich angerufen?	*Are there any calls for me?*

17. Nachrichten wiederholen und überprüfen

Haben Sie das?	*Have you got that?*
Können Sie das bitte noch einmal vorlesen?	*Can you read that back to me, please?*
Soll ich es noch einmal wiederholen?	*Shall I repeat that?*
Könnte ich einige Einzelheiten notieren?	*Could I take down some details, please?*
Einen Augenblick bitte. Ich möchte mir die Einzelheiten aufschreiben.	*Just a moment please. I would like to take the details down.*
Darf ich Ihnen alle Punkte noch einmal vorlesen, um sicherzugehen?	*May I just read back the details to you to make sure?*
Vielleicht habe ich Sie nicht richtig verstanden. Könnten Sie das bitte wiederholen?	*Perhaps I didn't understand you. Could you say it again, please?*
Ich bin mir nicht sicher, ob ich das richtig mitbekommen habe. Ich wiederhole.	*I' m not sure whether I got that right. I'll repeat it.*
Ich würde gerne sichergehen, daß ich alles richtig verstanden habe.	*I would like to make sure that I've understood that correctly.*
Darf ich Ihren Nachnamen buchstabieren, nur um sicherzugehen?	*May I spell your surname, just to be sure?*
Möchten Sie, daß ich alles noch einmal durchgehe?	*Would you like me to go over that again?*

Lassen Sie mich das noch einmal durchgehen.	*Let me go over that.*
Würden Sie den Preis bitte noch einmal wiederholen?	*Would you mind repeating the price?*

18. Auf einen Telefontermin beharren

Wann kann ich ihn erreichen?	*When can I reach him?*
Wann kann ich mit ihm sprechen?	*When can I contact him?*
Wie kann ich sie erreichen?	*How can I get hold of her?*
Können Sie mir sagen, wann sie da ist?	*Can you tell me when she'll be in?*
Ist sie morgen im Büro?	*Will she be in the office tomorrow?*
Könnten Sie mir bitte sagen, wann sie wieder zurück ist?	*Could you please tell me when she will be back?*
Wissen Sie, wann er zurück sein wird?	*Do you know when he'll be back?*
Kann ich ihn unter irgendeiner Nummer erreichen?	*Is there a number where I can reach him?*
Wann wäre es günstig, es noch einmal zu versuchen?	*When would it be a good time to try again?*
Wann ist es am günstigsten, zurückzurufen?	*When's the best time to ring back?*
Können Sie mir sagen, wann ich ihn am ehesten antreffe?	*Can you tell me when I am most likely to find him in?*
Wäre neun Uhr eine gute Zeit, um Tom zu erreichen?	*Would nine o'clock be a good time to get hold of Tom?*
Ich versuche es dann morgen noch mal.	*I'll try tomorrow, then.*
Ich rufe sie gleich morgen früh an.	*I'll call her first thing in the morning.*

19. Um einen Rückruf bitten

Könnten Sie Frau Child bitten, Bob Marley anzurufen?	*Could you ask Mrs Child to call Bob Marley, please?*
Könnten Sie Tom veranlassen, mich zurückzurufen?	*Could you get Tom to ring me back?*
Könnten Sie ihn bitten, mich unter meiner Privatnummer zurückzurufen?	*Could you ask him to phone me back on my private number?*
Sagen Sie ihm bitte, daß er sich mit mir in Verbindung setzen möchte.	*Please tell him to get in touch with me?*
Ich bin bis 3 Uhr Ihrer Zeit zu erreichen.	*I'll be available till 3 p.m. your time.*
Haben Sie eine Nummer, unter der wir Sie erreichen können?	*Do you have a telephone number we can contact you on?*
Sie können mich unter dieser Nummer erreichen.	*You can reach / call me at this number.*
Und wann wäre es für Sie günstig, daß Tom Sie anruft?	*When would it be a good time for Tom to call you back?*

Er ruft Sie an, sobald er zurück ist.	*He will get back to you as soon as he arrives.*
Wann würde es Ihnen passen?	*When would it be convenient for you?*
Würde Ihnen Dienstag um neun Uhr passen?	*Would Tuesday, nine o'clock be a convenient time?*
Sie können mich über das Autotelefon erreichen.	*You can contact me by car phone.*
Sie rufen mich doch an, wenn er zurückkommt?	*You'll give me a ring when he gets back, won't you?*

20. Was sagen Sie, wenn Sie zurückrufen?

Hier ist Fred Niemec. Ich sollte Herrn Slicer zurückrufen.	*This is Fred Niemec returning Mr Slicer's call.*
Tut mir leid, daß ich Ihren Anruf verpaßt habe.	*I'm sorry I missed your call.*
Tut mir leid, daß Sie mich nicht erreicht haben.	*Sorry you didn't get me.*
Hier spricht Tickersun. Man hat mir ausgerichtet, ich solle Sie zurückrufen.	*Tickersun here. I got a message asking me to call you back.*
Sie haben mir eine Nachricht hinterlassen, daß ich Sie zurückrufen soll.	*You left a message asking me to call you back.*
Ich bin froh, daß ich Sie erreiche.	*I'm glad I've got hold of you.*
Ich freue mich, daß es mir gelungen ist, Sie zu sprechen.	*I'm pleased I managed to get in touch with you.*

21. Sich für einen Rückruf bedanken

Ich bin froh, daß Sie so schnell zurückgerufen haben.	*I'm glad you called back so soon.*
Vielen Dank, daß Sie mich zurückrufen.	*Thank-you for returning my call.*
Danke für Ihren Rückruf.	*Thanks for calling me back.*
Danke, daß Sie zurückgerufen haben.	*Thanks for getting back to me.*
Ich weiß das zu schätzen.	*I appreciate it.*
Wir haben Ihren Anruf erwartet.	*We've been waiting for your call.*
Ich habe mich auf Ihren Anruf gefreut.	*I've been looking forward to your call.*

22. Falsch verbunden

Kein Anschluß unter dieser Nummer.	*Number unobtainable.*
Bedaure. Falsch verbunden.	*Sorry. Wrong number*
Tut mir leid. Sie haben falsch gewählt.	*Sorry, you've dialled the wrong number.*
Man hat Sie falsch verbunden.	*You've got through to the wrong number.*
Tut mir leid, dies ist die falsche Nebenstelle.	*Sorry, this is the wrong extension.*
Tut mir leid, aber dies ist nicht die richtige Abteilung.	*I'm sorry, but this is not the right department.*
Seine Rufnummer hat sich geändert.	*His number has been changed.*
Die neue Nummer ist ...	*The new number is ...*
Dies ist nicht die Abteilung, die Sie wünschen.	*This isn't the department you want.*
Diese Abteilung hat damit nichts zu tun.	*This department doesn't deal with that.*
Welche Nummer versuchen Sie zu erreichen?	*What number are you trying to get / reach?*
Welche Nummer wollen Sie haben?	*What number are you calling?*
Wen, sagten Sie, wollten Sie sprechen?	*Who did you say you wanted to speak to?*
Niemand dieses Namens arbeitet hier.	*Nobody by that name works here.*
Ich sollte unter dieser Nummer anrufen.	*Well, this is the number I was asked to ring.*
Sie können ihn direkt anrufen.	*You can dial him direct.*
Haben Sie seine Durchwahl?	*Have you got his extension?*
Entschuldigen Sie bitte die Störung.	*Sorry to have troubled you.*
Ich bin mit der falschen Abteilung verbunden worden.	*I was put through to the wrong department.*
Könnten Sie mich wieder mit der Vermittlung verbinden?	*Could you pass /hand me back to the operator?*

23. Der freundliche Gesprächsbeginn

Spreche ich mit Herrn Brain?	*Am I speaking to Mr Brain?*
Guten Morgen. Dr. Brain am Apparat.	*Good morning, this is Dr. Brain.*
Erinnern Sie sich an mich?	*Do you remember me?*
Ich habe gedacht, ich rufe Sie mal an.	*I thought I'd give you a call.*
Ah, Herr Brain, das ist aber eine unerwartete Freude.	*Ah, Mr Brain. This is an unexpected pleasure.*
Was für eine angenehme Überraschung!	*What a pleasant surprise!*
Nett, von Ihnen zu hören.	*How nice to hear from you.*
Es ist schön, wieder etwas von Ihnen zu hören.	*It's good to hear from you again.*

Wie schön, daß ich dich erreiche.	*I'm pleased to get hold of you.*
Nett, Ihre Stimme wieder zu hören.	*Nice to hear your voice again*
Ich habe schon die ganze Zeit versucht, mich mit Ihnen in Verbindung zu setzen.	*I've been trying to get into contact with you for some time.*
Hätten Sie vielleicht einen Moment Zeit für mich?	*I wonder / I was wondering if you could spare me a minute?*
Oder soll ich später noch einmal anrufen?	*Or shall I call back later?*
Ich hoffe, ich störe nicht.	*I hope I'm not disturbing you.*
Keineswegs, nicht im geringsten.	*Not at all.*
Tut mir leid, wenn ich Sie störe.	*I'm sorry to disturb you.*
Tut mir leid, wenn ich Ihnen Mühe mache.	*Sorry to trouble you.*
Habe eine Ewigkeit nichts mehr von dir gehört.	*Haven't heard from you for ages.*
Vielen Dank für Ihren Rückruf.	*Thanks for calling me back.*
Es war nicht einfach, Sie an das Telefon zu bekommen.	*It's been difficult getting hold of you.*
Hallo Tom. Wie geht es dir so?	*Hello Tom. How are you keeping?*
Wie geht es dir so?	*How are you doing?*
Wie geht's, wie steht's?	*How are the things?*

24. Was sagen Sie, wenn die Leitung schlecht ist?

Die Leitung ist leider schlecht.	*I'm afraid the line is bad.*
Wie bitte?	*Pardon? / I beg your pardon?*
Ich verstehe Sie nicht gut.	*I can't hear you very well.*
Ich kann Ihre Stimme kaum hören.	*I can hardly hear your voice.*
Es klingt, als wären Sie meilenweit weg.	*It's as if you're miles away.*
Tut mir leid, das habe ich nicht mitbekommen.	*Sorry, I didn't quite catch that.*
Können Sie mich gut hören?	*Can you hear me alright?*
Ich kann Sie kaum verstehen.	*I can hardly hear you.*
Könnten Sie bitte lauter sprechen?	*Could you speak louder, please?*
Hier ist ein fürchterlicher Lärm.	*There's an awful noise here.*
Könnten Sie bitte lauter sprechen?	*Could you speak up, please?*
Wir haben eine schlechte Verbindung.	*We've got a bad connection.*
Die Verbindung ist furchtbar schlecht.	*The connection is terrible.*
Die Leitung ist furchtbar schlecht.	*The line is terrible.*
Ich hoffe, Sie können mich gut verstehen.	*I hope you can hear me okay.*
Sie klingen sehr leise.	*You sound very faint.*
Ich kann nicht verstehen, was Sie sagen.	*I can't make out what you're saying.*
Das ist jemand in der Leitung.	*We've got a crossed line.*

Leider ist die Leitung schlecht. Könnten Sie das wohl wiederholen?	*I'm afraid the line is bad. Would you mind repeating that, please?*
Würden Sie die letzten Worte bitte wiederholen?	*Would you please repeat the last remark?*
Da ist ein schreckliches Nebengeräusch.	*There's terrible interference.*
Sind Sie noch dran?	*Are you still there?*
Mein Gespräch ist weg.	*I've lost my caller.*
Die Leitung ist tot.	*The line's dead.*

25. Wie Sie sich bei Verständigungsschwierigkeiten helfen

Ich fürchte, mein Englisch ist nicht sehr gut.	*I'm afraid my English isn't very good.*
Entschuldigen Sie, aber ich spreche nicht gut Englisch.	*Excuse me, but I don't speak English very well.*
Könnten Sie das bitte wiederholen?	*Could you repeat that please?*
Könnten Sie das noch einmal wiederholen?	*Could you say that again, please?*
Dürfte ich Sie bitten, das zu wiederholen?	*I wonder if you could say that again, please?*
Könnten Sie bitte langsamer sprechen?	*Could you speak more slowly, please?*
Entschuldigen Sie bitte, aber das habe ich nicht mitbekommen.	*I beg your pardon, but I missed that.*
Ich weiß nicht, ob ich das richtig verstanden habe. Ich wiederhole.	*I' m not sure whether I got that right. I'll repeat it.*
Meinen Sie November oder September?	*Do you mean November or September?*
Sagten Sie Hoover oder Moover?	*Did you say Hoover or Mover?*
Ich würde gerne sichergehen, daß ich das richtig verstanden habe.	*I would like to make sure that I understood that correctly.*
Entschuldigen Sie, ich wiederhole.	*I'm sorry. I'll repeat that.*
Können Sie mir folgen?	*Are you still with me?*
Könnten Sie das buchstabieren?	*Could you spell that for me?*

26. Was sagen Sie, wenn Sie unter Zeitdruck stehen?

Ich muß leider zum Schluß kommen.	*I'm afraid I'll have to cut this short.*
Ich stehe unter Termindruck.	*I'm hard pressed for time.*
Ich muß unser Gespräch in ungefähr 5 Minuten beenden.	*I've got to leave you in about 5 minutes.*
Ich muß mich nun verabschieden.	*Well, I'll have to say goodbye now.*
Tut mir leid. Ich kann jetzt nicht sprechen. Ich bin mitten in einer Verhandlung.	*Sorry, I can't talk to you now. I'm in the middle of a negotiation.*

Entschuldigen Sie, aber ich muß unsere Unterhaltung jetzt beenden. Mein Besucher ist eingetroffen.	*Sorry, but I have to end this discussion now. My visitor has arrived.*
Ich habe ein volles Programm.	*I've got a full schedule.*
Ich bin in Zeitnot.	*I'm very short of time.*
Ich muß nun aufhören. Ich habe in fünf Minuten eine Besprechung.	*I have to go now. I have a meeting in five minutes.*
Ich kann im Augenblick nicht sprechen. Ich habe Besuch.	*Sorry, I can't talk now. I've got a visitor.*
Tut mir leid Fred, aber ich hab's eilig. Ich muß jetzt Schluß machen.	*Sorry, Fred, but I'm in hurry. I have to finish our call now.*
Hör zu, so gern ich dich mag, ich muß jetzt aufhören.	*Listen, I'll love you and leave you now.*
Ich muß mich beeilen.	*I've got to rush.*
Kann ich Sie zurückrufen, wenn ich etwas mehr Ruhe habe?	*Can I phone you back when it's a bit more peaceful?*
Könnte ich Sie zurückrufen, wenn ich mehr Zeit habe?	*Could I phone you when I've more time?*
Und wann wäre es für Sie günstig, daß ich Sie anrufe?	*When would it be a good time for me to call you back?*
Wann würde es Ihnen passen?	*When would it be convenient for you?*

27. So schirmen Sie Ihren Chef ab

Ein Herr Smith ist am Telefon. Soll ich das Gespräch durchstellen?	*There's a Mr Smith for you on the phone. Shall I put him through?*
Ein Gespräch für Sie. – Sagen Sie, ich rufe später zurück.	*There's a call for you. – Tell him I'll call back later.*
Es ist ein Verkäufer. Nehmen Sie das Gespräch an?	*It's a salesman. Will you take the call?*
Ich habe einen Herrn Smarty am Apparat, der Sie unbedingt sprechen will.	*I've got a Mr Smarty on the phone who seems to be very keen on speaking to you.*
Herr Brown ruft aus Brüssel an. Soll ich verbinden?	*Mr Brown is phoning from Brussels. Shall I put him through?*
Ein Herr Smith möchte Sie sprechen. Soll ich das Gespräch auf Ihren Apparat legen?	*There's a Mr Smith for you on the phone. Shall I put him through to your extension?*
Frau Child ist leider nicht zu sprechen.	*I'm afraid Mrs Child is not available.*
Er ist gerade nicht im Raum.	*He isn't in at the moment.*
Herr Tickersun hat strenge Anweisung gegeben, nicht gestört zu werden.	*Mr Tickersun left strict instructions that he was not to be disturbed.*
Er kommt wahrscheinlich sehr spät zurück.	*He'll probably return very late.*

Ich schlage vor, Sie versuchen es morgen noch einmal.	*I suggest you try again tomorrow.*
Oder kann ich Ihnen vielleicht weiterhelfen?	*Or maybe I can help you?*
Könnte Ihnen vielleicht ihre Sekretärin weiterhelfen?	*Could her secretary help you?*
Möchten Sie mit jemand anderem sprechen?	*Would you like to speak to someone else?*

28. So könnte Ihr Chef reagieren

Sagen Sie ihm, ich rufe später zurück.	*Tell him I'll ring back later.*
Ich kann dieses Gespräch nicht entgegennehmen. Ich habe Besuch.	*I can't take that call. I've got a visitor.*
Fragen Sie ihn, wann er möchte, daß ich zurückrufe.	*Ask him when he would like me to call back.*
Könnten Sie das Gespräch für mich annehmen? Ich habe zu tun.	*Could you please answer the phone for me. I'm busy.*
Ich stecke bis über beide Ohren in Arbeit.	*I'm up to my neck at the moment.*
Vertrösten Sie ihn bitte auf später.	*Could you please put him off until later.*

29. Telefongespräche beenden

Ich störe Sie nun nicht mehr weiter in Ihrer Arbeit.	*I'd better let you get on with your work.*
Es war nett, mit Ihnen zu sprechen.	*It's been nice talking to you.*
Ich würde mich freuen, wieder von Ihnen zu hören.	*I'm looking forward to hearing from you.*
Es war schön, von Ihnen zu hören.	*Nice to hear from you.*
Vielen Dank für Ihre Hilfe. – Bitte sehr, nicht der Rede wert.	*Well, thank-you very much for your help. – Don't mention it!*
Ich bin Ihnen sehr dankbar für Ihre Unterstützung. – Gern geschehen.	*We're very grateful for your assistance. – You're welcome.*
Ich bin Ihnen sehr verbunden. – Keine Ursache.	*I'm much obliged to you. – Not at all.*
Kann ich sonst noch etwas für Sie tun?	*Anything else I can do for you?*
Gibt es sonst noch etwas (zu besprechen)?	*Will there be anything else?*
Ich glaube, das wär's einstweilen.	*I think that's it for now.*
Ich glaube, das wäre im Moment alles.	*Well, I guess that's all for now.*
Vielen Dank für Ihren Anruf. Lassen Sie mal wieder von sich hören.	*Thank-you for your call and keep in touch.*
Vielen Dank für Ihren Anruf.	*Thanks for ringing.*

Vielen Dank für Ihren Anruf.	*Thank-you for calling.*
Vielen Dank für den Anruf.	*Thank-you for the call.*
Vielen Dank, daß Sie uns angerufen haben.	*Thank-you for calling us.*
Sie hören von mir (am Dienstag).	*You'll be hearing from me (on Tuesday).*
Ich rufe Sie wieder an.	*I'll ring you again.*
Sie hören bald wieder von mir.	*I'll get back to you soon.*
Ich muß nun los.	*Well, I'll be off now.*
Bis heute abend.	*See you tonight.*
Mach's gut.	*Take care.*
Rufen Sie mal wieder an.	*Keep in touch.*
Einen schönen Tag noch.	*I wish you good-day.* (ironisch)
Auf Wiederhören einstweilen.	*Goodbye for now.*
Auf Wiederhören.	*Goodbye.*
Tschüs.	*Bye then.*
Wiederhören.	*Bye.*
Tschüs.	*Cheers.*
Bis bald.	*See you.*
Bis später.	*So long.*

30. Anrufbeantworter und Ansagen

Hier ist der automatische Anrufbeantworter der Firma Robotalot.	*This is the automatic answering machine of Robotalot.*
Dies ist eine Bandaufnahme.	*This is a recorded message.*
Unser Rufnummer hat sich geändert.	*Our telephone number has been changed.*
Sie erreichen uns unter 33 44 54.	*You can phone us on 33 44 54.*
Wählen Sie bitte 23 23 23.	*Please call 23 23 23.*
Dieser Apparat ist im Augenblick nicht besetzt.	*There's nobody here at the moment.*
Wir sind im Augenblick leider nicht erreichbar.	*Sorry, we can't be reached at the moment.*
Sie rufen außerhalb unserer Bürozeiten an.	*You have phoned outside office hours.*
Sie können uns eine Nachricht hinterlassen.	*You can leave a message.*
Wir rufen Sie baldmöglichst zurück.	*We ring you back as soon as possible.*
Sprechen Sie bitte nach dem Signalton.	*Please speak after the tone.*
Wir sind im Augenblick nicht erreichbar. Hinterlassen Sie Ihren Namen, Telefonnummer und eine Nachricht. Wir rufen Sie so schnell wie möglich zurück.	*Sorry we are out. But leave your name, number and message and we'll get back to you as soon as we can.*

Sie sind mit PELC verbunden. Unser Büro ist geöffnet von Montag bis Freitag zwischen 9 Uhr und 16 Uhr. Vielen Dank für Ihren Anruf.	*You are calling PELC. Our office is open from Monday to Friday from 9 a.m. to 4 p.m. Thank-you for calling.*
Die gewählte Rufnummer hat sich geändert.	*The number you have reached has been changed.*
Die gewählte Rufnummer hat sich geändert. Die neue Nummer ist ...	*The number you wanted has been changed. The new number is ...*
Kein Anschluß unter dieser Nummer.	*Number unobtainable.*
Ihr Anruf kann nicht ausgeführt werden.	*Your call cannot be put through.*
Bitte versuchen Sie es später noch einmal.	*Please try your call later.*
Überprüfen Sie die Rufnummer, und versuchen Sie es noch einmal, oder wenden Sie sich an die örtliche Auskunft.	*Please check the number and dial again or call your local operator.*

31. Sie möchten ein privates Telefon benutzen

Ich würde gerne meinen Mann anrufen.	*I'd like to ring up / call my husband.*
Dürfte ich Ihr Telefon benutzen?	*May I use your telephone?*
Entschuldigen Sie bitte, wo kann ich hier telefonieren?	*Excuse me, where can I make a telephone call?*
Entschuldigen Sie, dürfte ich bitte Ihr Telefon benutzen. – Aber natürlich. Bedienen Sie sich.	*Excuse me, may I use your phone, please? – Of course, go ahead.*
Gehen Sie in mein Arbeitszimmer, da können Sie ungestört telefonieren.	*Go into my study. You'll have some privacy there.*
Lassen Sie mich das Gespräch bitte bezahlen.	*Please let me pay for the call.*
Ich würde das Gespräch gerne bezahlen.	*I would like to pay for the call.*

32. Sie wollen ein öffentliches Telefon benutzen

Wo ist bitte die nächste Telefonzelle?	*Where's the nearest phone box, please?*
An der Ecke ist eine Telefonzelle.	*There is a phone box (US: telephone-booth) on the corner.*
Könnten Sie mir bitte Kleingeld für die Telefonzelle geben?	*Could you give me some small change for the phone, please?*
Könnten Sie mir ein paar Münzen für die Telefonzelle geben?	*Could you give me some coins for the phone?*

33. Hinweise in Telefonzellen

Nehmen Sie den Hörer ab.	*Lift the receiver.*
Werfen Sie das Geld ein.	*Insert your money in the slot.*
Es sind mindestens 10 Pence erforderlich.	*A minimum of 10 p is required.*
Warten Sie auf das Amtszeichen.	*Listen for the dialling tone.*
Wählen Sie die gewünschte Nummer.	*Dial the number required.*
Werfen Sie kein Geld ein. Diese Gespräche sind gebührenfrei.	*Do not insert money. These calls are free.*
Diese Nummer ist gebührenfrei.	*This is a free-phone number.*
Notrufe. Wählen Sie 999.	*Emergency calls: dial 999.*
Die Nummer hat sich geändert.	*The number has been changed.*
Wählen Sie zuerst die internationale Vorwahlnummer ...	*First dial the international code ...*
... dann die regionale Vorwahlnummer ohne die Null ...	*... then the area code minus initial '0'...*
... dann die Nummer des Teilnehmers.	*... then dial the subscriber's number.*

34. Telefonieren im Postamt

Kann ich nach München in Deutschland durchwählen?	*Can I dial straight through to Munich in Germany?*
Kann ich nach München durchwählen?	*Can I dial / get Munich direct?*
Ab wann beginnt der Nachttarif?	*What time does the cheap rate begin?*
Die Vermittlung hilft Ihnen.	*The operator will assist you in making the call.*
Könnten Sie mir bitte die Vermittlung geben?	*Could you please give me the telephone exchange?*
Ist dort die Bahnhofsauskunft?	*Is that the Central Station Information?*
Vermittlung, würden Sie bitte mein Gespräch nach München streichen?	*Operator, will you please cancel my call to Munich?*
Ich habe es wiederholt versucht, aber ich bekomme keine Antwort.	*I've tried again and again, but there is no answer.*
Die Verbindung ist furchtbar. Ich glaube, sie ist gestört.	*It's a terrible connection. I think it's out of order.*
Wir sind unterbrochen worden.	*We have been cut off.*
Geben Sie mir bitte die Störungsstelle.	*Please give me the operator. There's a fault on the line.*
Ich hätte gerne ein Ferngespräch nach Bristol.	*I'd like to make a long-distance call to Bristol.*
Ich hätte gerne ein Gespräch mit Voranmeldung.	*I'd like to place a person-to-person call.*

Telefon: I think it's out of order (geht nicht)

Ich möchte gern ein R-Gespräch nach New York machen.	*I'd like to make a reversed /transferred charge call to New York.*
Wie ist der Name des Teilnehmers?	*What is the name of the party/person you are calling?*
Können Sie mir eine Verbindung nach Zürich herstellen?	*Can you get me a line to Zurich, please?*
Wie lautet die Telefonnummer?	*What's the number, please?*
Wissen Sie zufällig die Vorwahlnummer?	*Do you happen to know the dialling code (am: area code)?*
Haben sie ein Telefonbuch?	*Do you have a directory/phone book?*
Ich brauche das Branchenverzeichnis.	*I need the yellow pages.*
Was kostet ein Ortsgespräch zum Flughafen?	*What does a local call to the airport cost?*
Ein Ferngespräch nach Heidelberg in Deutschland bitte.	*A long-distance call to Heidelberg in Germany, please.*
Muß ich lange darauf warten?	*Will I have to wait long?*
Könnten Sie mir die Nummer des Strandhotels geben?	*Could you give me the telephone number of the Strandhotel?*
Teilen Sie mir bitte mit, wieviel das Gespräch kostet.	*Please let me know what the call comes to.*
Ich möchte das Gespräch bezahlen.	*I'd like to pay for the call.*
Die Vermittlung ruft zurück und sagt Ihnen, wieviel das Gespräch macht.	*The operator will ring you back and tell you how much the call comes to.*
Wann muß ich die Münze einwerfen?	*When have I got to insert the money?*
Wenn Sie den hohen Signalton hören, müssen Sie Geld nachwerfen.	*When you hear the high-pitched tone, you have to insert more money.*
Vermittlung, ich bin unterbrochen worden. Können Sie mich bitte wieder verbinden?	*Operator, I've been cut off. Could you connect me again, please?*
Bei Unfällen wählen Sie 999.	*In case of accident dial 999.*

35. Anpiepsen und Faxen

Ich piepse ihn an. / Ich lasse ihn ausrufen.	*I'll page him.*
Ich schicke Ihnen ein Telex.	*I'll send you a telex.*
Ich schicke Ihnen ein Telex mit den neuen Preisen.	*I'll telex the new prices to you.*
Wir schicken Ihnen ein Fax.	*We'll send you a fax.*
Faxen Sie mir bitte Ihre Preisliste zu.	*Please fax me your pricelist.*

▷ wir sind unterbrochen worden: we have been cut off

36. Buchstabieren am Telefon

30 22	*three – O – double two*
01-4587665	*O – one – four – five – eight – seven – double six – five*

The British Telephone Alphabet

A –Alfred	H – Harry	O – Oliver	V – Victor
B – Benjamin	I – Isaac	P – Peter	W – William
C – Charles	J – Jack	Q – Queen	X – X-ray
D – David	K – King	R – Robert	Y – Yellow
E – Edward	L – London	S – Samuel	Z – Zebra
F – Frederick	M – Mary	T – Tommy	
G – George	N – Nellie	U – Uncle	

SCLÜSSEL ZU DEN ÜBUNGEN

CHAPTER I

EXERCISE 1

MBI, good morning. Doris Child speaking. Can I help you? 1
I' d like to speak to Mr Tickersun, please. 2
Who is calling, please? 3
This is Dr. Brain here. 4
I'm afraid Mr Tickersun is at a meeting. 5
Can I be of help? 6

EXERCISE 2

Sagen Sie, wer Sie sind.	Hello Brian. This is Tom speaking.
Fragen Sie, ob er etwas Zeit hat.	I wonder if you could spare me a minute.
Bieten Sie an, zu einer anderen Zeit zurückzurufen.	Or shall I call back some other time?
Sagen Sie, daß Sie im Auftrag von Herrn Tickersun anrufen.	I'm calling on behalf of Mr Tickersun, you know.

EXERCISE 3

Mimi: Satco Company. Good afternoon. Who is speaking? / Sorry, I'm afraid Mr Knut is not in his office. He's in/at a meeting. / As you wish. I'll tell Mr Knut that you have called. Goodbye.

CHAPTER 2

EXERCISE 1

I'll put you through / I'll transfer you / I'll connect you with

EXERCISE 2

British Rail, can I help you? 1
Excuse me, madam, could you put me through to the Lost Property Department? 2
Just a moment, please. 3
Sorry, the line's engaged. Can you hold or would you like to call again? 4
I think I'll try again later. When would be the best time to call back? 5

EXERCISE 3

Tom Smarty	**Jacky Brain**
Good afternoon. I'd like to speak to Mr Brain.	I'm sorry. He's still at the factory. Would you like to leave a message?
Yes please. I' m calling about the advert in the Late News. What would be a good time to call back?	The best time would be after eight o'clock. What did you say your name was?
Smarty, Tom Smarty.	Well, Mr Smarty, I'll tell my husband that you called.
Thank-you, Mrs Brain. Goodbye.	Goodbye.

EXERCISE 4

British Rail. Can I help you?	Mrs Sills here. Could you put me through to Lost Property?
Just a moment. I'm connecting you.	Thank-you.
Lost property. Can I be of help?	I'd like to enquire if someone has handed in my handbag.
Do you remember where you lost it?	In Victoria Station, I think.
And when was that?	Friday evening. At about 9 o'clock.
	All my documents were in it.

Documents? In that case I'll have to pass you over to my colleague. It's ringing for you.
Thank you.
John Smith speaking. My colleague told me that your handbag is missing. Could you describe it in some more details?
Sure, it's a small brown leather handbag.
What did you say your name was?
Sills, Susan Sills.
Could you spell that, please?
Es Ai double el es, Sills.
May I ask when you were born, Mrs Sills?
I was born on October 20th, 1948.
You are lucky, Mrs Sills. I've got your handbag in front of me on my desk.
Oh, great! I'll come right now and collect it.

CHAPTER 3

EXERCISE 1

TH: What seems to be the problem today? / BC: I'm afraid I must complain very strongly.

EXERCISE 2

Media Centre, good morning. What can I do for you? 1
I've got a serious complaint to make. The vacuum cleaner I bought yesterday doesn't work properly. 2
May I ask what the problem is? 3
Well, it doesn't suck in the dust. It blows it out. 4
I'm awfully sorry to hear that. That's really a nuisance. 5
Please accept our apology. 6
What are you going to do about it, if I may ask? 7
If you bring the vacuum cleaner, I'll look into it immediately. Of course, we'll pay for the taxi. 8
That sounds reasonable. I'll be along in an hour. Goodbye. 9
I'm relieved we managed to sort it all out. Please ask for Miss Roomy. Goodbye. 10

EXERCISE 3

I don't normally complain but this is really too much / I'm afraid I've got to make a serious complaint. / I really can't accept this kind of thing again. / I'm afraid I can't accept that. / I've been totally dissatisfied with your customer service so far.

EXERCISE 4

May I ask what the problem is? / I'm awfully sorry to hear that. / We owe you an apology for the delay. / I realise that this may put you in a difficult position. / May I explain the matter from our point of view? / We'll check the problem and call you back immediately / I'm sure we can sort this out.

EXERCISE 5

"Is that customer service? I've a complaint (to make). We ordered typing paper from you. That was a month ago. It hasn't arrived yet."
"Something has obviously gone wrong. We'll check the problem and call you back immediately."

CHAPTER 4

EXERCISE 1

1a I suggest that you apply. 2c I suggest asking for more information. 3c Wouldn't it be a good idea if you phoned the company now? 4b Wouldn't it be a good idea to ask for an interview? 5c What if we took a look at other ads?

EXERCISE 2

We advise you to pay; Well, may I suggest a compromise?

EXERCISE 3

Susan: Is that you, Tony? It's Susan here.
Tony: Hello Susan. How are you keeping?
Susan: The usual stress. Is Fred in? I've been trying to get hold of him for the last few days. It's urgent.
Tony: Just a moment. I'll see if he's in. (after a while) He' s coming. I had to wake him up. Well, Susan, it's been nice hearing from you. Keep in touch.
Fred: Hi, Susan. Haven't heard from you for ages. How are things?
Susan: Fine, thank you. I've been trying to get in touch with you for quite a while. Why didn't you call back? Didn't you get my message? Listen, I think I've found just the right job for you.
Fred: A job! Not again. You know I haven't recovered from the last one you found me.
Susan: It's always the same with you. Why not earn some money for a change? I'll be with you in a minute. I suggest you have a look over the advert. So long.

EXERCISE 4

How are you going/keeping? How are things/has life been treating you?

CHAPTER 5

EXERCISE 1

No doubt you have noticed Fred's six basic mistakes: 1. He did not identify himself. / 2. He did not address her by name. / 3. He did not say "good morning". / 4. He could not give the reason for his call. / 5. He wasted the receptionist's time. She had to ask him a lot of questions. / 6. He could not name the person or the department he wanted.

EXERCISE 2

May I ask your name? What's the purpose of your call?

EXERCISE 3

I'm afraid Mr Brain is not available at the moment. / I'm sorry, but Mr Brain is on holiday this week. / I'm afraid she is out of the office this week. / Mr Brain is away on business. / I'm sorry, Mr Brain is at a meeting. / He left strict instructions not to be disturbed. / He's in the middle of an interview. / He has got an important visitor. / Dr. Brain is very busy at the moment. /

EXERCISE 4

R: Schneider, IP Computers. Good morning. What can I do for you?
A: Good morning. Put me through to the head of customer services, please.
R: What did you say your name was?
A: Anton Sparbier. I'm one of your regular clients.
R: What's it in connection with, please?
A: I'd like to draw your attention to a defect in one of your models.
R: One moment, please, I'm putting you through.

EXERCISE 5:

1. Good morning. Can I help you? / 2. What is it in connection with? / 3. Sorry, I didn't catch your name. / 4. I'll check whether he can take the call.

EXERCISE 6

Are you going to take the call? Tell her that I've got a visitor.

CHAPTER 6

EXERCISE 1

Mimi's English corrected:

M: I hope so. I would like to speak to your boss, to Mister er ... Oh! now his name has slipped my mind.

M: No, Pardon was not his name. Wait a moment ... I remember his first name, Andrew. I met him in Paris at a computer trade fair.

M: I'm calling from Germany.

M: That's a good idea. My number is 116671. Thank-you very much/Thanks a lot. You've been most helpful.

EXERCISE 2

name /slipped	His name has slipped my mind.
memory /name	I've a bad memory for names.
need/ Mr Brain	I (really) need to speak to Mr Brain.
told / out	I'm told he's out today.
helpful	You've been most helpful.
welcome	You're welcome.

CHAPTER 7

EXERCISE 1

Describe the way to the Ritz: Leave the Station, cross Foster Square, walk along Field Street, turn right into Park Street, take the first left and you can see the hotel in front of you.

EXERCISE 2

Knox:	Good afternoon. I'd like to speak to Dr. Brain, if that is possible.	1
Child:	I'm afraid Dr. Brain is not available at the moment. Can I take a message?	2
Knox:	It's about that advertisement in the Late News.	3
Child:	I see. So it's in connection with the post of a salesman we've advertised, isn't it?	4
Knox:	Yes, that's it.	5
Child:	In that case I'll transfer you to the personnel department. Who shall I say is calling?	6
Knox:	My name is Knox, like Fort Knox in the States.	7
Child:	Hold the line please, I'm putting you through.	8

EXERCISE 3

Mimi: Yes, I learnt it at school.

Mimi: Of course. Go straight ahead and cross the park. From there you can already see the station. It's the big building in front of you.

CHAPTER 8

EXERCISE 1

Well done! / Full marks!

EXERCISE 2

Andrew: Could you put me through to Mr Halfar please?

Jane: I'm sorry he isn't in the company today.

Andrew: Could you take a message for him?

Andrew: Could you tell him ... Please ask him if ...
Jane: OK. I'll pass your message on to him.
Jane: You're welcome.

EXERCISE 3

I can take a message / Could you just let her know that...? / I'll give her the message as soon as she comes back

CHAPTER 9

EXERCISE 1

Mimi corrected: Sorry to interrupt you; It's impossible ; In the room opposite; completely naked; nonsense

EXERCISE 2

a) Tin Lizzy: Tommy, Isaac, Nelly, next word London, Isaac, double zebra, yellow
b) Robotalot: Robert, Oliver, Benjamin, Oliver, Tommy, Alfred, London, Oliver, Tommy
c) Brain: Benjamin, Robert, Alfred, Isaac, Nelly

EXERCISE 3

H: Robotalot. Good morning. What can I do for you?
S: I'm calling about your advert. I'd like to apply for your job and ...
H: Now just a moment ... for my job? But that is ...
S: Excuse me for interrupting you, but, you misunderstand. For the post of a salesman for your line of robots, of course.
H: You're lucky. We have been looking for someone for quite some time. Can I call you back when I've more time? What did you say your name was?
S: Spade, Sam Spade.
B: Let me spell it to make sure.

CHAPTER 10

EXERCISE 1

What did they say for... ?	**They said :**
Can I help you?	Can I be of assistance?
What else can I do for you?	How can I help you further?
It's about a new product.	It's in connection with a new product.
Could you possibly put me in contact with him?	Could you possibly put me through to him?
Sorry to interrupt you.	Sorry to break in.
The connection is bad.	The line is bad.

EXERCISE 2

appointment / cancel

EXERCISE 3

1c Sorry, I didn't catch your name. 2a I'm not sure if I got that right.
3b We've got terrible interference. 4a What did you say your name was?

EXERCISE 4

When would it suit you? When would it be a good time ? Would 5 p.m. be alright? Let's make it Wednesday. What about 6 p.m.? We could have a working dinner. Wednesday the first of May, at 6 p.m. at the Codogan.

CHAPTER 11

EXERCISE 1

This is the wrong number/department/extension

EXERCISE 2

What number are you calling? / Who did you say you want to speak to?

EXERCISE 3

Bob: Hello, could I speak to the information clerk, please?
Info: I'm sorry. You've got the wrong number. This is Blight's.
Bob: I don't understand ...
Info: What number are you trying to call?
Bob: British Rail. 01 926 47111.
Info: Well, we're 926 47711. Sorry to have troubled you.
Bob tries again:
Info: Passenger information. Good morning.
Bob: Could you give a few times, please? I'd like to arrive at about 6 p.m. in Glasgow.
Info: There's only one train and that arrives at 7.30 a.m. It departs from Victoria at 11.45 p.m.
Bob: Thank you. Goodbye

EXERCISE 4

Mimi corrected: Could you tell me how to get to Canterbury? This is the third time that I've got a wrong number. I wonder when I will get the right number. In this country everything is so complicated.

CHAPTER 12

EXERCISE 1

Would it be possible to leave a message? / Could you let him know that I'll call back tomorrow? / Would you pass a message on to Mr Shark?

EXERCISE 2

Mr Shark is away on business / is not available / is at a meeting / is out of the office.

ERCISE 3

Mimi: I have recently heard that you are offering a new domestic robot.
Mimi: Excuse me, if I break in /I'm interrupting. This is a long-distance call. I'm calling from Germany. Just one question: can the robot cook?
Mimi: Very good. Can it also make leg of pork with sauerkraut ?

EXERCISE 4

J: Sorry, Andrew, Dr. Halfar is still on holiday. Can I take a message?
A: Would you please tell him that I'm going to Glasgow to Domestic Services on the third and ...
J: Just a moment, please, I'd better note this down.
A: ... so I won't be back for three days. Ask him if has got the new brochures already and if he could send them to Domestic Services. The address is on my desk. Have you got that?
J: I'll repeat to make sure ...

CHAPTER 13

EXERCISE 1:
1e; 2f; 3d; 4c; 5a; 6b

EXERCISE 2
I'm hard pressed for time; I've got a visitor; I'm in the middle of an interview; I've got a train to catch ; I've got to attend a meeting; I've got a full schedule

EXERCISE 3
I wonder if you can you spare me a minute? I must tell you how wonderful your Beef Bourguignon was. Can you let me have the recipe, please?

EXERCISE 4
B: Ah, Mr Goodman. This is an unexpected pleasure.
G: Good morning Mr Brodie. I'm really glad to get hold of you.
I wonder if you can spare me a minute.
B: Certainly. What can I do for you?
G: I hope I'm not disturbing you, but it's urgent.
Could we put off our meeting to Thursday?
B: That suits me fine. But I'm afraid I'll have to cut this short.
I've got to attend our weekly production meeting. See you on Thursday, then.

CHAPTER 14

EXERCISE 1
1f; 2a; 3b ; 4e; 5c; 6d

EXERCISE 2
First he booked; Then he changed the booking; Finally he cancelled the booking

EXERCISE 3 :
1d; 2c; 3a; 4b

EXERCISE 4
Mimi's mistakes corrected: Good morning. I'm calling to see if you have got a room for me. Could you please speak more slowly? I'm from Germany, you know, from the Waterkant. One night. How much is the room? Excuse me. I'm afraid I've missed that again. I think I'd better come along personally. Cheers.

CHAPTER 15

EXERCISE 1
I'm afraid I have to go now/ to cut this short/ to stop this.
It's been nice talking to you/ to hear from you/hearing your voice again.
You'll be hearing from me. Keep in touch. I'm looking forward to hearing from you. I'll phone you when I've more time. I'll get back to you soon. I'll ring you up again. You'll be hearing from me.

EXERCISE 2
1c; 2d; 3b; 4a

EXERCISE 3
S: Hello, John Shark here. Excuse me for calling during your lunch break.
Do you remember me?
N: I beg your pardon, who is calling?

S: Shark, John Shark. The Purchasing Director at Hospital Services.
N: Shark?... Yes, of course I remember you. I'm sorry, I didn't recognise your voice.
S: I'd like to invite you for dinner. We could sign the contract on that occasion,
N: I'm afraid, I'll have to have a look in my diary first. Unfortunately I don't have it with me at the moment.
S: No lame excuses, Fred!

EXERCISE 4

I'm awfully sorry, I'm not quite sure how to put this, sir, but I'm afraid I'll be late this morning.

CHAPTER 16

EXERCISE 1

Penta Hotel. Can I help you? – I'd like to speak to Mr Goodman. I'll just see if he's in. His key is not here, so he's in his room. – I'll just put you through.

EXERCISE 2

How about having a celebration? Why not take an early flight? How do you feel about that? I suggest going international. Might it be an idea if you learnt German? What about selling in Germany?

EXERCISE 3

Brain here. / I'm pleased to get hold of you. / I've been trying to get in contact with you for some time. / It's in connection with X. / Now to the point. I'm phoning because... / I can't talk to you now. / I'll phone you when I have more time.

EXERCISE 4

It's in connection with X. / It concerns X. / The reason why I'm calling is ... / I'm ringing about X. / I'm calling to ask ... / I'm phoning because ...

CHAPTER 17

EXERCISE 1

The Secretary
I'm afraid I can't put you through.
I suggest you try again tomorrow.
He has left instructions not to be disturbed.
Please calm down.
His phone is ringing for you.

Andrew Goodman
I can't make it.
Couldn't we postpone this anniversary?
Let's fix another date then.

Fussy Pot
I advise you to put me through immediately.
Get off the phone!
I'm looking forward to our weekend.

EXERCISE 2

I've been holding for ages; You put me through to the wrong department; You gave me the wrong extension; I can't hold any longer

EXERCISE 3

Mimi's English corrected.
I'm Mimi Salkes from Aurich. I want to buy one of your robots. Would you please put me through to the director? And since it is a long distance-call from Aurich, Germany, I'd be obliged, if it didn't take too long.

Well, perhaps you can. I'd like to know if your robot would be able to feed my cat and to play with him. But you should know that my Pussy is a very wild and big cat.

EXERCISE 4

Please, be patient, it won't take long. I'm only doing my job. I'm doing my best. Please, calm down.

CHAPTER 18

EXERCISE 1

Of course, and very well, too. Do you mean Herrn Geiger? If you don't know his name, how can you have an appointment?

EXERCISE 2

Bye; Bye then; Goodbye then; Good bye for now.

EXERCISE 3

I didn't get that.	I didn't catch what you said.
Could you connect me?	Could you put me through?
Could you put me through?	Could you transfer me?
It is about the robot.	It's in connection with the robot
I've been looking forward to your call.	We've been waiting for your call.
Will there be anything else?	Anything else I can do for you?
I'll get back to you soon.	You'll be hearing from me.

EXERCISE 4

... spare me a minute; ... for ages; It's Fred again, I hope I'm not disturbing you. Not at all ...

CHAPTER 19

EXERCISE 1

Lines can be crossed; awful, bad; terrible

EXERCISE 2

he phoned up his friend / you'll have to speak up / I can't hear a word you're saying. / the line is terrible, I can't make out what you're saying. / I can hear the caller distinctly /

EXERCISE 3

hear him well; understand a word; make out what she says; hear what he says; hear her clearly; hear his voice

EXERCISE 4

I've heard a lot about your business skills / We would like to compliment you on your work

CHAPTER 20

EXERCISE 1

I'll have to say goodbye now. / When would (it) be a good time to call you back? / You'll give me a ring when you get back, won't you. / You can page me there and I'll get back to you immediately. / Well, so long. Bye for now. / Take care. Keep in touch.

EXERCISE 2

What do I have to do to get you to put me through – wait till Christmas? / I can't keep waiting any longer. / I've been holding for ages. / I haven't got all day.

EXERCISE 3

Who am speaking to? / We've (got) a bad line/connection. / Didn't you recognise my voice? / You'll call/ give me a ring/phone me up as soon as you're back, won't you? / This a long-distance call. / Is that you, Niemec? / So long.

CHAPTER 21

EXERCISE 1

Can I help You? Can I be of assistance? At your service. How can I help you? Can I be of help? What can I do for you?

EXERCISE 2

Fred Niemec speaking. / I didn't catch your name. / Now just a moment, sir. / I wish you good-day.

EXERCISE 3

Bob Late violates the following rules: 2 5 7 8